I love how Natalie has given us a glimp
into her own heart and story, and a vi
to sing the song God's given each of us
friend of Natalie's. Now I'm happy to ca

   SHAUNA NIEQUIST, author, *Bread*

We all have to go on a journey to find our voice; we have to resist the temptation to become an imitation and be willing to allow what's within to be heard. In this book my dearest friend shares from her beautiful heart how your voice not only needs to be heard but how it can become a voice for those who have none. Natalie's honesty is refreshing, her message is liberating, and her passion is evident—to use her voice to help others find theirs. I am so grateful for the gift within these pages because when we all dare to find our voice, the world can begin to hear what freedom really sounds like.

   CHARLOTTE GAMBILL, pastor, author, speaker, and cofounder of
   "Dare to Be"

In her book, *Finding Your Voice*, Natalie inspires us by vulnerably sharing her own personal struggles with pain, doubt, and insecurity. She also brilliantly challenges us to awaken our own voice and to live out the design and purpose Jesus has called us to. Natalie, ever so gently, invites us to join her in finding our song and singing it *boldly*!

   SHELLEY GIGLIO, Chief Strategist, sixstepsrecords; Cofounder,
   Passion Conferences/Passion City Church

Finding Your Voice shares an amazing reflection of how intimately God wants to connect with each of us. From her own personal journey of wrestling through pain and fear, Natalie shares how she came to the powerful realization that God has given each of us a unique voice for his glory. The voice that God gave you is powerful, it is precious, and it is enough!

   LISA BEVERE, Messenger International, bestselling author, *Lioness
   Arising*, *Kissed the Girls and Made Them Cry*, and *Fight Like a Girl*

You are precious, beloved by God, and have been given a song from him that only you can sing. In *Finding Your Voice*, Natalie will help you discover that *song* and so much more. I'm so excited for you to read it!

> **KARI JOBE**, singer, songwriter

Natalie has one of the most beautiful and compelling voices I have ever heard. She has pushed through many barriers to let it be heard, and now she teaches us how to do the same thing.

> **SHEILA WALSH**, author, *The Longing in Me*

I have loved Natalie and her music for a long time. This new offering is an intimate look into her life and processes and pain that is not only interesting but also truly helpful for any woman looking to find her voice.

> **ANNIE F. DOWNS**, bestselling author, *Looking for Lovely*
> and *Let's All Be Brave*

Natalie has touched a generation. She radiates hope, strength, and faith. We who have been blessed by her songs are now blessed to read her book.

> **MAX LUCADO**, pastor and bestselling author

I learned long ago that finding your voice does not mean learning how to sing. It's so much more and so much deeper than that. From someone who took the long way to find her voice, I am so proud of Natalie, my dear sister-friend, in how she has bravely walked the path of freedom in finding her voice. She's certainly helped me find mine throughout the years of our friendship, and I know she will help you find yours through this new book.

> **SANDI PATTY**, most-awarded female vocalist in gospel
> music history

FINDING YOUR
VOICE

FINDING YOUR
VOICE

WHAT EVERY WOMAN NEEDS TO LIVE
HER GOD-GIVEN PASSIONS OUT LOUD

NATALIE GRANT

 ZONDERVAN®

ZONDERVAN

Finding Your Voice
Copyright © 2016 by Natalie Grant

Requests for information should be addressed to:
Zondervan, *3900 Sparks Dr. SE, Grand Rapids, Michigan 49546*

ISBN 978-0-310-34939-6 (audio)
ISBN 978-0-310-34476-6 (ebook)

Library of Congress Cataloging-in-Publication Data

Names: Grant, Natalie, 1971–author.
Title: Finding your voice: what every woman needs to live her God-given
    passions out loud / Natalie Grant.
Description: Grand Rapids: Zondervan, 2016.
Identifiers: LCCN 2016013687 | ISBN 9780310344735 (softcover)
Subjects: LCSH: Oral communication—Religious aspects—Christianity.
    Music—Religious aspects—Christianity. | Christian women—Religious life.
Classification: LCC BV4597.53.C64 G73 2016 | DDC 248.8/43—dc23 LC
    record available at https://lccn.loc.gov/2016013687

Published in association with Maximum Artist, 4219 Hillsboro Pike, Suite 234,
Nashville, TN 37215.

Cover design: *Micah Kandros*
Cover photo: © *conrado / Shutterstock®*
Author photo: *Dominick Guillemot*
Interior design: *Kait Lamphere*

First printing July 2016 / Printed in the United States of America

CONTENTS

For Bernie—
no other voice has been a greater example of true love,
encouragement, and understanding in my life. I love you so.

For Charlotte—
your gift of creativity and the way you use your voice
helped to shape this book from the start.
Forever grateful for you, my friend.

Chapter 1

LEARNING TO LISTEN

———————— ✍ ————————

*M*y voice has been my purpose, my ministry, my career, my life. I've always wanted my songs to soothe and comfort those who are hurting, to speak truth and love to the broken, and I've been incredibly humbled and blessed to be a part of God's work in this way.

But there was a moment years ago when I was voiceless that I will never forget. A moment that I could not speak at all, but I *could* listen.

It all started when I was watching an episode of *Law & Order: SVU* in my home in Nashville. The episode was about human trafficking, and I had never seen it this closely before. As I sat among my throw pillows on my comfy couch in my world-class city, I was growing increasingly uncomfortable. Even in the fictional context of the show, the truth struck me. I was aghast at the exploitation of women and children, stunned by the callous acts of abuse perpetrated by heartless people seeking only profit and pleasure.

By the time the credits rolled, I was wrecked.

How could this abomination exist? How could women . . . children . . . be so marginalized and diminished to tools of pleasure of the most abhorrent nature?

How did I not know about this? What could I do?

Not content to wonder, I searched online for organizations that fight human trafficking. I found a phone number and called one, asking what I could do. They invited me to go on a trip with them to India so I could see with my own eyes this crime against humanity. I was off to "save the world"—or so I thought. In my head, I played out numerous scenarios of my headlining benefit concerts that would surely be a cure-all for these enslaved women.

I was packing for my campaign, feeling very proud of my generous and compassionate spirit, when God yanked the reins from my over-zealous hands, as if to say to me, "This isn't your show just yet. We're doing this My way."

Just days before we were to board the plane, my vocal cord hemorrhaged during a concert. Improper singing technique and a relentless schedule caused the tiny blood vessels surrounding my vocal cords to burst, leaking blood into the vocal cord. Such an injury is a singer's worst nightmare, and not only that, it seemed to come at the *worst* possible time. Ordered to complete vocal rest—no singing, no talking, no sound at all—the images of my valiant tour to save the world were dashed. I couldn't yet see how God would be able to use me without my unique gifts and talents. *What good was a singer without a voice? Where was my platform now?* I wondered. Here I thought my mission was about to begin, and now I was completely unarmed. My singing voice had been my lifeline, my defense, my purpose; but at that moment, I was without it. I couldn't see how God could use a voiceless vocalist.

To be honest, I considered canceling the trip.

It hadn't yet occurred to me that perhaps my true voice had nothing to do with singing at all. Up to that point in life, I had limited my own capacity to do good in this world to music, not knowing and not yet seeking to discover if God had different, bigger, deeper plans for my life. I sincerely wanted to serve Him and to use my gifts and talents in ways that honored Him, but my life had become so cluttered with obligations and expectations, I had forgotten how to listen. In the past, I'd often considered the concept of hearing God's voice as something mystical and put an inordinate amount of pressure on myself to hear it and be in His will. I often felt like a disappointment or failure if I couldn't discern it. My self-doubt then led to fear that I might stray to the right or left and just mess up everything.

I was at a crossroads. I could either bemoan the situation of silence or embrace it as a learning opportunity. It wasn't easy, but I opted for the latter. I chose to have a teachable spirit—to learn how not just to hear, but to listen to God's voice all over again. And I decided to go to India after all.

It was one of the best decisions I've ever made.

Looking back, I know that even though the doctor had ordered it, the Lord silenced my voice for that trip. He enabled me to hear His voice and the voices of those who had been silenced for too long. As I listened, I began to hear His still, small voice.

A SILENT JOURNEY

*S*he didn't make a sound. She wasn't screaming or asking for help. She was staring silently and almost vacantly through the metal bars. For a brief moment, we locked eyes. Even then, I couldn't process what I was seeing.

Through a second-floor window in the middle of Mumbai's red-light district, I saw a child who couldn't have been more than six, locked in a cold, metal cage. The sight floored me.

Even more devastating, though, was the utter lack of hope and resignation I sensed in her eyes as if she were reconciled to the fact that this was her lot in life. At a tender six years of age, this child's spirit was broken, just one of the millions of victims of human trafficking around the world.

Peering into her silent hell, I was stunned. I grabbed my husband's hand, and he saw what I saw. Side-by-side, we became witnesses to one of mankind's most heinous atrocities. Even more abhorrent, she wasn't alone.

They were as young as five. Tiny, beautiful, broken, terrified. Their eyes were sad, heavy, like they were carrying an overwhelming weight. Girls, children, bought and sold like property. Ravaged over and over with no defense. Like a walking nightmare.

They were silent. They hadn't been able to speak for themselves in years.

Their voices extinguished by fear, tossed around in a maelstrom of injustice, choking in a fire of depravity that they didn't start.

I couldn't help but wonder, Where was God in this? Where was the Voice of the Redeemer, speaking and acting on behalf of these young girls?

And then, out of the void created by evil emerged the faintest sound of hope. With my ears tuned in more acutely to this quiet rustling, the noise grew stronger, louder, and clearer. Then, as if everything else in the world had gone quiet, the sound became a distinct Voice uttering a singular word—*You.*

God had not abandoned these girls. He had not backed away, allowing this injustice to go on forever. He had sent help. He had sent others, like those in the organization that had brought me on this trip to India, to represent and restore the voices of so many who were preyed upon by corruption.

And now, He wanted to send me.

He had shaped inside of me a heart that was meant to be broken by the horror I was seeing. He had developed a platform and a sphere of influence in my life that He had now given a very clear purpose. I was Natalie Grant—recording artist, award-winning musician, performer. I made my living using my voice. I felt God asking me, would I be willing to use my voice to serve these women? Right then and there in the dusty streets of Mumbai, heavy with the weight of pain and hopelessness around me, I became a different Natalie Grant: the advocate, the abolitionist, the messenger of peace.

I can't say that everything came clearly into focus at that moment, but Mumbai was a turning point for me. Even though I was in Christian music, I had focused mainly on success. In choosing a singing career, I had genuinely wanted to honor God and help people find the hope of Jesus through the music I was singing. However, I also desired recognition that I was great at what I did, letting my position on the chart dominate my thoughts. On this trip, I began to see and become convicted that my voice was never meant simply to entertain; God gave me my voice to do the work of the Redeemer. There was a greater plan at work—a plan that required me to become smaller to see His greater works come to fruition.

My true voice, my God-given purpose, hadn't been lurking in a shadow or elusively escaping me all my life. It had been right in front of me the whole time. I had simply never been quiet or still long enough to hear it. Only when I learned to listen did my inner monologue morph into a dialogue in which I was finally assuming my God-given role.

Replaying the events and particular circumstances that had led me to that moment of revelation, I could see with increasing clarity the precision of God's timing and prompting. From my very first breath, God had been at work, crafting me to be a singer, a mother, a wife, and a minister. Over the years, He further cultivated within me a sense of compassion and a desire to serve the world . . . somehow. Mumbai began to show me how that might look.

If I were to guess, you've probably been in a state of crisis over where God was calling you a time or two yourself. Maybe you've wrestled with going back to work after the birth of a child. Perhaps you've walked away from, put on hold, or lived with a sense of guilt over a relationship you weren't sure was right. Or possibly, much like me, you thought you were living in the will of God and using your voice the way you were meant to when it was taken away. Maybe you were let go from a job you had really believed in or you didn't pass a qualifying exam, or someone important to you betrayed your trust.

If lost opportunity has you feeling broken or frozen, seeking but not finding God's direction, perhaps it's time to demystify what it means to hear from God.

THE STILL, SMALL VOICE

*W*hen we are born, our voice is the first sign of life. Parents, doctors, and nurses are tuned in, listening for the first cry. Eager to hear how well the lungs and heart are working . . . eager to know that the baby is aware and alert. Parents everywhere hold this moment as sacred in their memory.

We enter this world hard-wired to communicate with our voices. It's as natural as breathing. Over the next few years, the cries become words, which become sentences, which soon become conversations. By age seven, children can understand between 20,000 and 26,000 words.[1]

Clearly, we were created to be heard.

But we were also created to hear.

We weren't intrinsically born with dialects and colloquialisms ingrained into our brains. We acquire them from our surroundings. When we're young, we don't have much power over those surroundings. In terms of what they hear and what they don't, newborns and toddlers are at the mercy of their parents or caretakers.

Consciously or not, as we get older, we have more and more control over what we're hearing and processing. Very basic life choices can influence what we hear, what we process, and how we then respond.

As a musician, I'm used to being heard, but I'm only as good as my ears. Everything about my performance—my pitch, my tone, my dynamics, my timing—is predicated on what I hear. If I don't listen well, I'll be off. If I'm distracted, I'll miss entrances and cut-offs, and you can forget about nailing harmonies or other voice parts.

If anyone should understand the importance of listening, it's me. When I was in Mumbai, though, I realized I'd lost my focus. I'd been in Christian music for about five years at that point, and things were going pretty well, but I hadn't had a major breakthrough yet. I loved what I did, but a desire for success drove me. I was frustrated and a little confused as to why things hadn't taken off. I'd become too consumed with my rankings to realize why things weren't working.

India brought everything back into focus. It was the first time in a long time that I had been truly quiet. In the absence of my audible voice, I was finally able to hear. In my stillness,

I was able to listen. With my ears and my heart open, I heard something—a Voice of reason, of sanity, of purpose.

A Voice that said, *I've been waiting for you. There's work to be done.*

At that moment, my eyes were opened. The Lord hadn't set me on this path so I could win awards or sell records. He hadn't given me a voice just to entertain people. He had a much grander plan in the works. But until I was still enough, quiet enough to hear His direction and leading, there was no way I could fulfill the calling on my life or ever find my true purpose—my true voice.

That pivotal encounter with God saved my career and my life. More so, the foundation He laid would save an untold number of lives that I didn't even know existed yet. In the years since that visit, I've founded my own anti-trafficking organization to help launch, expand, and improve aftercare programs in India, Moldova, Cambodia, and the United States.

God had plans for me, just like He does for you.

I thought those designs began and ended with music. I couldn't have been further from the truth. But until God could break through and call my heart to attention, I couldn't be an instrument for His work. God had to get me beyond me so I could begin to see His plan for my life.

I had to learn to listen all over again.

Who knew that these lessons would take me to the other side of the world?

Every day, I thank God for awakening my heart to my true voice. As a mother of three daughters, I want to speak wisdom, kindness, faithfulness, and purpose into their lives. I want to give them a foundation from which to see God's will for them and to hear His voice in their own hearts and lives. I want them to be secure enough to be still. I want them to know how to listen.

Created in God's image, we should strive to be like Him in every way, so our voices should echo His. The only way to do so is first to hear His voice.

But do you know what you're listening for?

It's easy to say that you're pressing into God and that you're seeking His face and His will—especially when you're on stage singing about Him. It's another matter entirely to make your pursuit of His voice a daily, practical, tangible thing.

My hope for you is that this book can give you the tools, the perspective, perhaps even the motivation to be still enough to listen to His voice, and furthermore, to trust it and then follow it. Don't think you can do it perfectly . . . I didn't. It wasn't that I never had trouble hearing God again or that I had perfectly tuned my heart to all that the Lord had for me and my life. Far from it!

But later in life, even when depression crept in and I wrestled with who I was as a mother and a woman of God, the lessons I had already learned were present enough in my heart and mind to guide me through the dark nights.

I have spent many days unsure of myself and unclear about the merit of my voice in the world of entertainment, ministry, or justice. On those days, I have to make myself listen harder and more intently than ever before. That's when I have to dig deeper into the Bible. I believe that Scripture is God's word for our lives. It is the foundation for everything we do and say and hold true. While I believe that God can give us a word individually from our circumstances, it will never be anything outside the bounds of Scripture.

That is why, as I approached the idea of a book about finding your true voice—the whole package of your God-given identity, passions, and unique talents—I knew that it had to be saturated in the Word of God. There's one particular story from the Word of God that has been foundational for me and the message of this book.

"WHAT ARE YOU DOING HERE, ELIJAH?"

I love the story of Elijah being called to the mountain to listen for the voice of God.

But we've sanitized this story a lot in modern Christianity.

This whole notion of a "still, small voice" is usually taken out of context and, while it makes for a touching sentiment, told in such a way that removes the impact of that moment.

If you remember, Elijah wasn't just hanging out, waiting peacefully for a word from heaven.

He was running for his life.

He had just slaughtered the prophets of Baal, the false god ascribed to by two of the cruelest, craziest characters in history—King Ahab and Queen Jezebel.

Queen Jezebel didn't earn her storied reputation by happenstance. She was cruel and she was after Elijah. She had every intention of avenging the lives of her slaughtered prophets. 1 Kings 19:3 says, "Elijah was afraid and ran for his life."

Keep reading. Elijah may be a lot more like you than you realize.

> Elijah was afraid and ran for his life. When he came to Beersheba in Judah, he left his servant there, while he himself went a day's journey into the wilderness. He came to a broom bush, sat down under it and prayed that he might die. "I have had enough, LORD," he said. "Take my life; I am no better than my ancestors." (1 Kings 19:3–4)

Have you ever been there? Have you ever just had enough?

Have you ever wondered what is the point of your life and your voice in the first place?

When we look around, so often all we see is failure and fear and insurmountable odds. Elijah had just angered the most powerful and evil woman in the world. She had endless resources and countless ways to end his life.

This great prophet saw no way out. He was done.

Again, keep reading:

> Then he lay down under the bush and fell asleep. All at once an angel touched him and said, "Get up and eat." He looked around, and there by his head was some bread baked over hot coals, and a jar of water. He ate and drank and then lay down again. The angel of the LORD came back a second time and touched him and said, "Get up and eat, for the journey is too much for you." So he got up and ate and drank. Strengthened by that food, he traveled forty days and forty nights until he reached Horeb, the mountain of God. (1 Kings 19:5–8)

Looking back at your life, can you think of times when God supplied you with sustenance? When a meal was waiting or a check arrived in the mail? What about when a smile came your way at just the right time?

We serve a God of heavenly heights who crafted this physical world we live in. He knows when we're hungry and thirsty. He knows when we can't walk another step. He is as corporeal a God as He is spiritual. And He loves to provide spiritually and physically for His children.

As you think about peeling back the layers of your life and uncovering your true purpose, your true voice, it may seem overwhelming to you. There may be too much pain to work through. Maybe there's just too much damage.

I'm not going to tell you that it's in your head, nor am I ever going to dismiss someone's pain or history as unimportant or fabricated. What I am going to suggest is that God knows exactly where you are and the condition that you are in. He knows what you need to complete the journey. And He does provide.

God had to heal my body and prepare my heart before He could lead me to India. All He needed was for me to let Him. Be honest with yourself, with God, and be willing to let your walls down enough to let some healing begin. Drink some water. Eat some food. Get some rest. Take care of yourself; let others take care of you as you prepare for the journey ahead. And then, keep reading:

> There he went into a cave and spent the night.
>
> And the word of the LORD came to him: "What are you doing here, Elijah?"
>
> He replied, "I have been very zealous for the LORD God Almighty. The Israelites have rejected your covenant, torn down your altars, and put your prophets to death with the sword. I am the only one left, and now they are trying to kill me too."
>
> The LORD said, "Go out and stand on the mountain in the presence of the LORD, for the LORD is about to pass by."
>
> Then a great and powerful wind tore the mountains apart and shattered the rocks before the LORD, but the LORD was not in the wind. After the wind there was an earthquake, but the LORD was not in the earthquake. After the earthquake came a fire, but the LORD was

not in the fire. And after the fire came a gentle whisper.
(1 Kings 19:9–12)

Do you think Elijah was a little thrown by that first question? *What am I doing here?! I'm following you! You made me bread and sent an angel and led me here!*

That would have been my response. It's not Elijah's. Reading this, I even wonder why God included the conversation in this passage. An all-knowing God knew very well why Elijah was where he was. He had no reason to ask. But I suppose it's there for us to learn what conversing with the Lord looks like. Perhaps it's also to teach us how to evaluate where we are in life and why. If nothing else, it certainly establishes the gravity of Elijah's situation. He is the only one left alive.

He is alone.

God's great prophet, who has been pursuing His God with fervor, finds himself at the top of the most-wanted list, and the odds aren't good.

What happens next appears so odd and beautiful to me and affirms that His ways are not our own.

He tells Elijah to go out and wait for Him.

And then a wind came through that *tore the mountains apart.*

I've watched a lot of Weather Channel specials on crazy natural disasters. I've never seen a wind rip a mountain apart and shatter rocks.

Elijah did!

And then an earthquake AND a fire! Talk about when it rains it pours. First he's running for his life from man, and now nature seems to have turned on him. Why? Well, we don't know. There are no grounds for conjecture on these bizarre weather systems beyond what the Scripture says—God was not in them. He didn't seek to further attack Elijah. Coming to him gently, He whispered peace to Elijah's battered heart. His method was compassionate but purposeful.

I don't think it would be easy to hear a whisper in the midst of all that was happening around him. If I'd just experienced a rock-shattering wind, earthquake, and fire, I'd be pretty rattled. I don't know if I'd be able to hear a whisper above the sound of my palpitating heart—at least not until I had calmed down considerably.

I think that's maybe what God was going for. He needed Elijah to listen to Him and calmly act with wisdom. Elijah couldn't do that if he were in a frenzy. Elijah needed to physically still his mind, body, and heart in order to receive further instruction. God's communication device—a whisper—required him to do just that.

He requires the same of us.

To trust in the face of despair.
To be still in the midst of chaos.
To go out and wait for Him.
To be His in a world that pulls us in every
   other direction.

That's when we find our voice.
That's when the pinnacle moments in life occur.

Have you ever read the rest of that chapter? Do you know what God was whispering to Elijah? He was telling him about the prophet Elisha. Where to find him, how to approach him, and how he would be not only Elijah's helper but the one to take Elijah's place.

I'd say that was a significant whisper.

At the end of the day, our ultimate hope lies in Jesus'

sacrifice on the cross. His desperate heart's cry is for your heart. His greatest desire is to be with you forever. He loves you that much.

But the greatness of being His doesn't end there. When we try to give our hearts and our lives to Him, the rewards are beyond comprehension. He has created each and every one of us for a particular purpose and a very specific goal.

He's created you to be a voice of hope and love to someone. Someone is waiting to hear from you. But first, you have to hear from the One who created your inmost being, just as He set the stars in the sky and the planets into orbit. You've got to be able to listen to a gentle whisper and believe what it says about you and what you have been created to do.

Your voice is glorious.

Your potential is monumental.

You just have to be ready to hear, to learn, to train, to care, and to trust in the One who walks on water and brings the dead to life.

It may not be an easy journey.

You may have to face things from your past and even things inside your own heart that are painful and messy.

You may have to be silent for a while.

It will be a sacrifice. But it is one of eternal return.

Your voice is alive.

Your voice matters.

You simply must be still enough . . . for long enough . . . to hear from the One who created your voice, so that when that still, small voice gently whispers for you to go, you'll be ready.

ALL THE WORLD'S A STAGE

*S*hakespeare famously said that all the world is a stage. With the rise of Facebook, Twitter, Pinterest, Instagram, and more, there is rarely a moment in our lives that isn't recorded or shared. Often, of our own choosing, we are "on stage" twenty-four hours a day.

While that's not necessarily a bad thing, it does have enormous implications on the kind of life we live and the kind of person we are. Now, the social pressure to be successful, marry well, raise brilliant children, and look stylish in skinny jeans while doing it all is exponentially higher. Now, instead of our immediate family or circle of friends and colleagues, the entire world is offering their opinion on who we should be. "Having it all" has become more of a cultural mandate than an ideal. Individual aspirations become narrowly defined qualifications. Dreaming becomes striving. Before we know it, the joy we once found in our hopes and plans for the future is replaced by stress and a frenetic lifestyle that promises the world, yet leaves us empty.

Many of us (myself included) find ourselves compromising our authenticity for the sake of conformity. We put our dreams to sing, write, fundraise for a good cause, adopt, [*or fill in the blank*] on hold to maintain a personal profile online, in person, or on paper that culture has deemed acceptable. Somewhere along the way, we can convince ourselves that the opinions of others trump our self-perception. In a society that has placed a premium on belonging, the risk of pursuing our own path seems too great. Suddenly, having it all becomes having what everyone else has.

Maybe you take that corporate job you're dreading because it offers premium health insurance.

Maybe you lay down a microphone, a paintbrush, or a pen to pursue a "real career."

Maybe you go on that extreme diet or buy those clothes you really can't afford or even surgically alter your appearance in order to look the part.

But here's something to think about . . . What part? What role are you convinced that you must fill? Can you remember what's at the root of all this desperation to be more or better?

Are you afraid that people will see the real you behind your polished persona? Are you so focused on what you think you should be that you've forgotten who you are? Have your tireless efforts to look connected to society created a disconnect with yourself?

Personally, I find it all too easy to be so caught up in the chaos of life, so overwhelmed with being busy that the only way to get through is to go on autopilot. Life becomes less about living and more about surviving. In the din, not only is my own voice hard to discern—there are moments when I barely remember the sound of it.

It's tempting to chalk up this culture of disconnect to social media or technology or the changing demands on women in the twenty-first century, but that's not only a narrow assumption; it's a dangerous one. When we start blaming external circumstances for our internal conflict, we minimize the consequences of our actions. We also unwittingly declare that we don't believe our Creator can handle our situation.

Of course, this isn't a twenty-first-century problem. Go back in time—way back—to Moses. He was called to speak and free his people. He doubted his ability to do so.

Scared to follow his call, Jonah found himself in the belly of a whale. (Let's hope that's not a recurring outcome.)

Esther was afraid to go before her own husband to plead for the life of her people.

Rahab must have been frightened as she defied her own people with a scarlet rope.

Mary faced the possibility of death due to her divine pregnancy. She went on to raise a son she knew would be taken from her one day.

Perhaps one of the most poignant and heart-wrenching stories of all is that of Peter. He feared the crowds, he feared the death he knew Jesus would imminently suffer, and he denied Him. Three times. In turn, he denied his true self—a redeemed, new creation.

Does that make him a bad person? No worse than any other human.

Were Eve, Moses, Peter, or Mary weak, disobedient, and doubtful? Yes. Just like the rest of us. But God didn't abandon them. Even when they feared the inevitable, God was with them every step of the way to remind them of the truth—they were not alone, they were loved, and they had been chosen to share a message with the rest of the world that only they could tell.

You and I are the same. Even when we cower from our callings, God will not fault us for our fears nor will He make us face them alone. He keeps pace and even goes before us to remind us of our truth—we have a voice unlike anyone else's, and we are equipped with all that we need to change the world in unprecedented ways.

It took me a while to realize this in my own life. Despite a healthy dose of rejection at the beginning of my music career, God never let me forget the ministry tool He had placed within me at the moment of conception—my singing voice. Over the years, I've learned different techniques and strategies to honor that gift, care for it, enhance it, and share it. As I've done so, God has continued to bless me, taking the hope within my songs to the very ends of the earth.

He longs for you to encounter and share your own gift—your own voice—as well. Whether or not you sing, speak, teach, write, stay at home with your children, or engage in another vocation, the voice he placed inside of you the rest of the world needs to hear. This precious commodity should never be hidden or ignored. We are daughters, mothers, sisters, wives, endowed with traits and tendencies that only women have.

Whether through a microphone or not, your voice—your call, your purpose in life—has a unique message, and God has provided practical guidance in Scripture to equip you to use it. If you're anything like me, though, it's often hard to quiet ourselves to read, much less understand and apply lessons learned. Thus, we retain our identity as Christians but live a life going through the motions, leaving us unfulfilled and those around us uninspired.

The great news is that it's never too late to begin turning things around.

Even when you are unsure of yourself, He isn't.

Even if you don't know the song yet, you still have a voice.

Let's go find it.

Chapter 2

TRUSTING YOUR POTENTIAL

————————— ဢ —————————

I f you ever hope to truly discover your voice and live your passions out loud, you first have to believe that your voice deserves to be heard. Even more, you have to trust that God has created you for a very specific, beautiful, unique purpose. He knows every intonation of your voice. He knows the cadence of your conversations. He knows the untapped potential within you waiting to be unleashed. He knows the beautiful future that lies ahead of you—a future that He wants you to not only count on but also to embrace with everything you have.

In short, He believes in you, and He wants nothing more than for you to believe in Him and His beautiful creation— you. Before you can do that, however, you have to untangle the web of destructive expectation and paralyzing uncertainty. What better place to start than, "Once upon a time . . ."

BACK TO NEVERLAND

D o you remember when Wendy and Peter Pan reunite at the end of the classic fairy tale? Peter is still young and flying and free while Wendy can no longer remember how to fly. Her simple explanation . . . "I grew up."

Do you remember when you forgot how to fly? When the world of princesses and castles and happy endings became a memory amongst a reality of hard relationships, pragmatism, and disappointment?

When we're young, we are plied with the ideal of happy ever after. It imprints upon us and finds a home deep within our subconscious. As we grow up, however, the message shifts. Culture still endorses that dream but also reminds us just how far away we are from it. And then the messengers offer us potions, products, wardrobes, procedures, and gadgets that promise to deliver the fantasy as long as we can pay up. There's no shortage of additional methods that can be purchased to numb our hurt feelings when we fall short yet again.

That is not the life God intended for us to live. Please hear me when I say that I don't liken God to a benevolent Walt Disney in the sky, nor are our lives supposed to be fairy tales with all happy endings. Rather, I'm suggesting that we serve a God of the impossible. He is a loving God who wants good things for His children. He is a God who desires us to serve Him with a child-like faith.

But many cultural messages reprise this story.

In a recent study by the Barna Group, practicing Christian women were eleven times more likely to admit they felt inferior when comparing themselves to other women via social media.

Inferiority breeds doubt.

Doubt distorts conviction.

Without conviction, you can't fully invest your belief in anything. And when you can't define your beliefs for yourself, culture, media, peers, and others will define it for you. For better or worse, external forces mold the way you perceive the world and yourself. Generic parameters established by people or institutions that don't necessarily know anything about you constrain your voice before you've even had a chance to hear it.

The cultural measuring stick of perfection tells you to be a princess, a size zero, a good cook, a mother, a wife, a blogger, a Pinterest all-star, and a CEO.

All positive things, but unrealistic, not to mention a bit one-dimensional.

If you are truly foraging in the depths of your heart and soul—past and present—for your authentic voice and calling, why limit yourself to surface-level ideals when you could be surrendering to and growing towards eternal bliss with a limitless God?

I'll be the first to admit that I've fought against feelings of inadequacy, incompetence, and insignificance. Even in my childhood, I knew I had a special talent for singing, but I bought into what the world around me was selling. I almost didn't allow myself to believe my dream was possible. So I did what I thought was sensible: going to college and studying elementary education to become a teacher.

Though teaching is an admirable profession, I quickly discovered I wasn't created for it. Not until joining a singing group called Truth in my third year at university did I begin to resonate with what I was hearing from God. I never heard Him speak audibly but recognized His voice in my spirit. When I started to do what I loved to do, what God had created me to do—operating fully in my gifting—I began to understand more clearly God's call on my life.

I've made so many mistakes in my life and am humbled every day that despite every shortcoming, God has still chosen to use me as a mouthpiece for Him.

It doesn't make sense. It's not logical. Then again, our God doesn't abide by laws of human logic or constraints. One look at His chosen disciples gives me more than enough evidence that God has always been in the business of using the least of these for His greatest cause. The ones that society has tried to silence or marginalize are those to whom He gives a megaphone.

There's no better example of this in Scripture than the work God chose to do through Peter. "And I tell you that you are Peter, and on this rock I will build my church, and the gates of Hades will not overcome it" (Matthew 16:18).

Peter got a shout-out in the previous chapter as well, and there's a reason he figures so prominently in my mind. History mainly remembers Peter as the solid rock . . . the one at the very foundation of our faith. All of that is true.

But sometimes we forget who Peter really was. This man who knew Jesus Christ on earth nearly better than anyone, who carried the movement of the Church following the crucifixion, was just as human as you and I are. In two epic moments, Peter revealed that even he had to fight to believe the miracle of who God is and what that meant about who Peter was. Let's revisit the stories of Peter's brief walk upon the water and his denial of Jesus. Chances are, you'll begin to see yourself in between the lines of Scripture. Incredulous as these stories may seem, they are just as relevant and compelling today as they ever have been.

WALKING ON WATER

If we are to truly invest our hearts and base our lives on Scripture, it has to be more than a story to us. I have to have a baseline for my life. Without it, I have no solid foundation from which to live, love, question, doubt, believe . . .

Walking on water has become a catchphrase and convenient superpower for our contrived heroes. It's right up there with flying carpets and Superman. We don't understand it. We can't necessarily prove it, so we label it a useful myth.

No wonder we have such a defective faith mechanism. If we shelve the examples and events that occur in the Bible alongside Marvel superheroes, we are removing the credibility of our one unshakable eternal foundation.

As Christians, we've been taught about the miracle of Jesus walking on water. It's a great VBS story and contains some good memory verses, but how often do you sit down and soak in and ponder this miracle?

> A strong wind was blowing and the waters grew rough. When they had rowed about three or four miles, they saw Jesus approaching the boat, walking on the water; and they were frightened. But he said to them, "It is I; don't be afraid." (John 6:18–20)

These guys were three or four miles out to sea. MILES! And out of the darkness, a figure emerges walking on the waves. A man they work with, walk with, live with is defying all that they understand about the physical world. Who wouldn't be astounded?

The disciples weren't just surprised or caught off guard. They were terrified! They didn't even recognize the figure to be Jesus until He addressed them.

To add another dimension to all of this, scroll back a few verses. The disciples were in the boat in the first place because they were leaving the gathering where Jesus fed five thousand people.

> Jesus said, "Have the people sit down." There was plenty of grass in that place, and they sat down (about five thousand men were there). Jesus then took the loaves, gave thanks, and distributed to those who were seated as much as they wanted. He did the same with the fish. (John 6:10–11)

That's right. The feeding of the five thousand is one of Jesus' most profound and talked about miracles. The disciples were there! They saw the little boy's loaves and fishes. They saw the hungry throng. They even carried the baskets to collect the leftovers.

Despite it all, however, they couldn't wrap their head around the possibility that Jesus could be striding towards their boat. Take that in. These men were privy to practically every miracle Jesus performed here on earth. Yet when it came down to fear or belief, their humanity won out . . . with a minor exception.

> "Lord, if it's you," Peter replied, "tell me to come to you on the water."
> "Come," he said.
> Then Peter got down out of the boat, walked on the water and came toward Jesus. (Matthew 14:28–29)

When I think of all these miracles and the way Jesus lived with such humanity in His time on earth, I easily disconnect my life, my generation, my personhood from this other world that exists in Scripture. However, because our God was fully God and fully man, I realize I have to decide every day to believe that what seems impossible, isn't. The best way I've found to go about it is to put myself there. I pray for an open heart and focus on the details of the text until I can see myself in the story. I try to connect the intangible with the tangible.

So join me—and Peter—for a moment. Even if you don't buy the story precisely as Scripture has recorded it, let's suspend reality for a bit. Press pause, and allow yourself to believe that Jesus did, in fact, walk on water. Believe also that Peter got out of the boat and for just a moment had the faith to meet Jesus on the waves.

Better yet, think about the last time you were at the beach. Do you remember the sound of the waves? The salt in the air? Was your skin sunburned? Were you thirsty? Remember the sting of the wind and that ever-present sense of sand that annoys you until you make it back home to a real shower in a building not sitting on a beach.

Or have you been on a boat in rocky seas? How did the pitch and yaw of the ship make you feel? Were you nauseated? Seasick? Did you wish that you were anywhere else?

Think on all that. And for a minute, close your eyes, breathe deeply, and let that scenario play out in your head . . .

Where did you go? Were you on the ocean? What did you smell? Who was with you? Make it personal. Make it your own.

Now, go back there and imagine Jesus standing before you—walking to you on the waves, while the storm continues to rage, waving to you to get out of the boat . . .

What do you do?

Is this just too incredulous or unbelievable to begin to accept? Are your eyes playing tricks on you? Are you suddenly suffering from some psychological breakdown?

Can you let yourself believe that it is real?

And yet, it is. Your Messiah is calling you to leave safety

and join Him in the chaos on the waves. He really thinks that you can walk on the water too.

What are you going to do?

You really just have two choices here—belief or doubt, trust or fear.

Fear has dominated much of my life. More times than I care to admit, I've allowed fear to establish a stronghold in nearly every aspect of my life. From my marriage and motherhood to my career and many things in between, I have been afraid to fail, afraid to disappoint and, at times, afraid to even move. That kind of fear is paralyzing and makes belief of any kind seem all but unreachable. I don't trust what I fear.

I flee what I fear.

God knows this instinct inside of me. Fight or flight wasn't something created by scientists. It wasn't an invention of modern humanity. Fight or flight was woven into our being along with the capacity to love or hate, to care or turn away, to believe or doubt. We were created with free will.

How many times are the words "do not be afraid" uttered in Scripture? Believe it or not, variations of that phrase appear 365 times in the Bible—one for each day of the year. It's no coincidence. God knows your fear and my fear just as He knew how terrified Mary would be. He anticipated Joseph would be skeptical, at best, possibly livid, and undoubtedly afraid. Jesus perceived His disciples' fear in that boat upon that stormy sea. He could hear Peter's pounding heart. He read the thoughts that must have been racing through Matthew's or Mark's mind. He understood that despite witnessing one of the greatest miracles in the history of the world . . . the feeding of five thousand people . . . they were going to doubt and let their fear cloud their faith. Even after all they'd seen, belief wasn't going to come easily or naturally to them.

Similarly in our lives, God knows that despite the many blessings, the many giftings He bestows upon us, we're always going to find something to be afraid of or some excuse to quiet the voice He's placed within us. We can easily fill our minds with doubts that will make us question, muffle, and in some cases, abandon the message He wants us to share. There will always be a reason to run and a shadow in which to hide.

It's impossible, however, to outrun His watchful eye and gentle hand. As fast as we try to run to a safe place, God's not a God who gives up easily. He is jealous for us.

He is jealous for YOU. And He yearns to hear that beautiful voice of yours resound through the song of your life. No one else in all of history sounds like you. No one else can satisfy the role you're meant to play.

Despite knowing every single thing we've ever done or ever will do, every single thought we have thought or will think, He passionately pursues us. Even when there is an ocean between your heart and His, He will tame every tempest, wave, and current to hold your heart close to His. He sustains us in the storm; and in our darkest, most pitiful or agonizing moments, His grace is enough. His grace is perfected in us when we are at our weakest. Our shortcomings attract His perfection. Even our fallacies shine a spotlight on His strength, love, and perfect salvation.

I have to think that Peter knew all of this. Standing by Jesus' side for years, he heard Him preach countless times. He had heart-to-heart talks by the fire with the man who broke his fishnets with His abundant provision. Peter was as close to Jesus Christ as any human being in history.

Perhaps all of those things came together in that one perfect moment of faith when Peter defied the wind and waves and threw his leg over the boat. In spite of his friends' warnings and his own knowledge of the ocean and sailing, which probably told him it wasn't smart to hop out onto the water. At that moment, none of that stood against his God. Nothing could pluck him from the loving, firm, eternal embrace of his Savior.

So he walked on the water too.

> "Lord, if it's you," Peter replied, "tell me to come to you on the water."
>
> "Come," he said.
>
> Then Peter got down out of the boat, walked on the water and came toward Jesus. (Matthew 14:28–29)

What a moment: The perfect love of your perfect Savior so fully came alive within you that you literally stood on the sea, eyes locked with your loving Creator.

I can only wonder at the euphoria that moment must have been in Peter's heart. I think about the birth of my children . . . when these miracles of life were birthed from my womb. Out of me—flawed, messy me—came these perfect, beautiful babies. Those were the most abundant, undeserved outpourings of grace and joy I've ever known.

I love to picture God relishing that moment with me.

In a way, it's even more precious to know that His pride and joy in me weren't dampened by His full knowledge of me and my sinful, unworthy heart. He knew how quickly my humanity, my fallen nature, would creep back in, distorting my faith and devotion. Yet, even knowing my depravity—what was, is, and is still to come—His pure and unconditional love enveloped me.

Peter's moment didn't last long. Even as he stood on the water, arm's length from Jesus incarnate, fear won out. The wind was too strong. The waves were too rough. His eyes were too blistered from the stinging salt. And he fell. "But when he saw the wind, he was afraid and, beginning to sink, cried out, 'Lord, save me!'" (Matthew 14:30).

I always hated that part of the story. It's almost as though the superhero didn't make it in time . . . or the knight in shining armor turned out to be anything but heroic. This was Peter. He was the first disciple! He was the rock! Yet, his faith faltered, prompting Jesus to say to him what must have felt like a kick in the stomach: "Immediately Jesus reached out his hand and caught him. 'You of little faith,' he said, 'Why did you doubt?'" (Matthew 14:31).

Peter must have been devastated. I would have been. These words were coming from the man, the cause, the God for whom he had abandoned his entire life. And yet, belief was still a battle . . . but a battle worth fighting.

As painful as it was to hear those words from Jesus, notice the first part of that verse. When Peter started going down, Jesus' first reaction was not of chastisement. His first move was a hand reached out. When Peter began going down, Jesus was immediately by his side with a literal lifeline. It was an action of mercy, grace, and provision. It was an action that perfectly met Peter's weakness.

Before Jesus offered correction, He waited until Peter felt safe. He didn't let him drown to teach him a lesson. He didn't even make him suffer. His response was immediate. His care was perfect. In that raging sea, at that moment, Peter was in an unshakable position. From that place—one of security and assurance—Jesus proceeded with the refining process and the hard questions.

This tells me two things. First, Jesus isn't out to get you. His love for you dictates His every move in your life. No matter how difficult His lessons may be, He is with you and shaping you for His glory. He is never letting go. "Be strong and courageous. Do not be afraid or terrified because of them, for the LORD your God goes with you; he will never leave you nor forsake you" (Deuteronomy 31:6).

Second, it tells me that the refining will probably hurt, but it won't overtake us. No matter how often we mess up or fall short, we'll never exhaust His supply of forgiveness, grace, and mercy. Even when we think we've got it all figured out and don't need Him or His hand upon our lives, God doesn't throw His hands up like a frustrated parent. Just look at Jesus on the water—His hand is stretched out and open. He doesn't condemn. He doesn't push. He loves and forgives and teaches—completely, unconditionally, eternally.

That said, it's not a one-and-done process—not for Peter, and not for us. Despite the magnitude of that experience, Peter's most infamous mistake was yet to come.

RIGHT VOICE, WRONG VOICE

I've always wondered if Peter replayed the water-walking incident in his head when Jesus laid the Last-Supper bombshell in his lap—that he would very soon deny Jesus three times.

> But Peter said to Him, "Even though all may fall away because of You, I will never fall away." Jesus said to him, "Truly I say to you that this very night, before a rooster crows, you will deny Me three times." Peter said to Him, "Even if I have to die with You, I will not deny You." All the disciples said the same thing too. (Matthew 26:33–35 NASB)

Perhaps there was a part of him that panicked at Jesus' words . . . a voice inside his head suggesting that his lack of faith had tainted his relationship forever.

A voice saying he'd brought this on himself.

A voice saying the past had stained his future.

A voice saying he was unworthy of this unmerited favor.

The conversation begins with Peter making a bold statement of allegiance and ends with the same promise.

Don't you think it's a bit odd that Peter felt the need to verbalize that? For me, I usually make my good intentions overtly known when I am either trying to hide something, deny something, or convince myself of something.

No one can ever know what Peter was actually thinking at that moment, except for Christ. But we all get to see how things played out just a few hours after their meal.

Peter and John and James had gone to the Garden of Gethsemane to pray with Jesus, oblivious of the nightmare that was to unfold that night.

And then it happened. Jesus was seized in the garden. Peter fought back, taking a swipe at the ear of one of the Roman guards. Jesus promptly healed the guard and then told Peter to drop his sword.

So he did.

His Savior was being led away in chains, beaten at every turn, and Peter was utterly helpless to defend Him or do anything to help.

The night goes on. Jesus is accused of blasphemy. Everyone must have known where it would all lead. The disciples seemed to have a pretty good idea. You don't hear much about them the rest of the night.

Until Peter is questioned. Once, twice, three times—three different people claim to have seen him with Jesus. They knew he was a friend, a colleague, a confidant. They knew Peter belonged to Jesus.

And then Peter broke his word and, undoubtedly, his own heart.

Once, twice, three times, he denies even knowing Jesus.

That night, fear won out.

Peter had the chance to throw himself at the mercy of God and stand by Jesus until the bitter end—which is what he had promised he would do less than twenty-four hours before. But when push came to shove, Peter saw Jesus' blood. He saw the bruises. He watched the torture of his Savior begin, and it was just too much. His humanity reacted naturally—it reacted in fear.

I wonder where Peter went for the rest of that night. Do you think he was able to sleep? I wonder if he confided in anyone else about all that had happened, or did he slink away in solitude, too ashamed to whisper his own deception to another. I wonder if he was even able to pray.

Talk about rock bottom. It doesn't get much worse than that. Much like many other failures, our worst seems to bring out His best.

God didn't see a washed-up, could-have-been disciple. He didn't see a liar or a coward.

He saw a rock. He saw the foundation of His church.

He'd seen it from the beginning. He knew what was going to happen. He knew Peter would fail. Yet His grace was more than sufficient for the tasks that lay ahead.

Peter was His man. Peter was His choice, and God held on to him zealously. It didn't matter how much the evil one tried to distort Peter's convictions or Jesus' perception of this man. It didn't matter that Peter lost his battle to believe; God had already claimed the victory—for Peter, for me, and for you.

The search for your voice begins and ends at the cross. That's where our doubt, shame, anger, and failures were washed away. Covered by His blood, we are worthy—worthy to love, to speak, to be heard. Worthy to pursue our passions and dreams guilt-free. We no longer have to acquiesce to the whims of popular culture or the lies that saturate society, telling us who we're supposed to be. Telling us just what kind of "ever after" we should pin our hopes on.

We are free to pursue passions, cultivate talents, and live out loud because of whose we are. We belong to the One who believes in you and me, who calls us forgiven, loved, and valued.

He gave each of us a voice and a message and was so convinced that we could fulfill the plans He has for us, He sacrificed His Son so we could have a chance to see them through.

Read that again.

God believes in who you are—your accomplishments, values, and dreams—with such intensity that He sent His only Son so YOU might live abundantly and with holy purpose.

No matter how far you fall, much like Peter, God will complete the good works He began in you. He only asks for your trust. His arms are open wide.

It's time to take a step forward in faith, to walk on the water and believe that you can do anything through Him.

Chapter 3

FINDING YOUR THRIVE ZONE

———————— &c ————————

I'll never forget my first year of college when I auditioned for a summer music ministry team. I had chosen to go to this small Christian school just outside of Seattle because of their exceptional music program. Their summer ministry teams had come through my church over the years when I was growing up, and it made me think I should go there to study education and in the summers travel and sing like they did.

I had always sung harmonies and lower parts, so I auditioned as an alto. Two days later, I got a slip under my door saying I had made it as a first soprano. I thought they had made a mistake. I ran to the music building, found the director, and let him know. He told me it was no mistake.

"You are a soprano," he had said. "You just don't know it yet. You can sing higher than you know."

He let me know it would take some practice (he was right!), but he saw potential in me that I didn't see in myself and began stretching me and showing me that I was capable of so much more than I had previously thought.

Before we go further, it's helpful to understand what types of voices there are. For women, in general, you are either a soprano, mezzo-soprano, alto, or contralto. Each part has a unique quality, function, and purpose within any given piece of music. You fall into one of these categories based on several criteria, but of utmost importance is your range. Vocal range is the set of notes between and including the highest and lowest notes you can hit. Within your range lies a specific span of notes that trained singers refer to as "tessitura."

Do you know how people talk about their comfort zone? The tessitura is even better than that. It's your *thrive* zone—your unique vocal range where you truly shine. Your sweet spot.

Too often, however, many women wish their voices were different than they are, much like brunettes who want to be blondes or short gals who wish they were tall. Many spend a lifetime trying to reach up or down into a tessitura that was never theirs to begin with.

Granted . . . it's definitely possible to expand your vocal range. With intense training and effort, you can add an octave or more to your range. The drawback here is the amount of time that must be invested to alter your natural voice. It can take years to create a new range which has a quality equal to the one you were born with.

The process can be tedious, exhausting, frustrating, and discouraging. It can also be dangerous. If you continue forcing your voice to reach notes it wasn't meant to hit, over time, you may do a lot of damage. And for what? Bragging rights?

Trying so hard to be something you're not deprives you of the joy of singing the range for which your voice was created. It deprives the world from ever hearing the beauty of your authentic voice.

Beyond that, focusing intently on the technical aspects of singing or playing can prevent you from connecting with the emotional impact of a song. If you're worried about hitting the high note at the end of the bridge throughout the song, you're missing out on the story of the verse and chorus that precede it. I once heard Brian Johnson from Bethel Church encourage musicians to find the key they are most comfortable either playing or singing. For guitar players, he suggested using a capo so as to be able to play in the key with the most familiar and comfortable fingering. (A capo is a nifty little device that guitar players can use to change the key of their instrument to one that they prefer to play in.)

For singers, he advises transposing a song to the key that would allow for the maximum impact upon delivery. The power of a song resides in its presentation. If the musician is nervous or uptight, the audience will be as well. If he or she is fidgeting with the mic cord until that high note comes and goes, chances are the audience isn't going to hear much of the song or the message it carries. They're going to be wondering if you're going to crack. Suddenly you are the displaced focus of the performance, drowning out your own song.

Today's culture often works the same way, especially for women. Society has defined for us "the lead" voices, celebrating women who are beautiful, thin, well-educated, financially secure, good mothers and wives.

And many of us want to be like these ideals who are lifted up. Why wouldn't we? These women seemingly have it all together. They're the mom at the soccer games who still had time to take a shower and dry her hair. They're the co-worker with the detailed memos and expense reports that are never late. They're the lady who Instagrams pretty portraits, perfectly posed and captioned.

It's classic "grass-is-greener" thinking.

We focus on becoming who we want to be or think we should be instead of who God made us to be. When our plan falls through or doesn't measure up, we easily write ourselves off as failures for not being some elusive ideal, though it was never who we were supposed to be.

For me, I so often universalize even the slightest failure. If I am late picking my kids up from school or blow up at them in a moment of frustration, in my head, I become the worst mother in the world.

Following my self-diagnosis, I withdraw or become cynical. Essentially, I diminish who I am and who I can be to others because I'm mad at myself. Too often, I let fear or worry erode my trust. At times, I have such a fear that God isn't going to fulfill His promises to me that I adopt a mind-frame of wanting or needing to control everything.

To write that so plainly, I grimace a bit. My babies became toddlers who huffed away from Mommy when they didn't get what they wanted. Kind of uncomfortable to realize that Mommy does the same thing!

So what do we do? For me, it begins with noticing my own habits. I've learned enough along the way to know that if I'm forcing something to happen that isn't going to happen, it's probably because my approach is wrong. If I'm spinning my wheels somewhere, there's a good chance I haven't consulted God or even considered His timing. More likely than not, I'm trying to fit my square end into a round hole, too frustrated or distracted to think about why things aren't working.

A BIG PROMISE, A BIG MISTAKE

If ever there were an example of being stretched beyond, and ultimately finding, their comfort zone, Abraham and Sarah would be it. Theirs is one of the most incredible biblical stories of faith being strained to its very limit.

When Abraham was relatively old, God promised him something that must have been inconceivable.

> "Sovereign LORD, what can you give me since I remain childless and the one who will inherit my estate is Eliezer of Damascus?" And Abram said, "You have given me no children; so a servant in my household will be my heir."
>
> Then the word of the LORD came to him: "This man will not be your heir, but a son who is your own flesh and blood will be your heir." He took him outside and said, "Look up at the sky and count the stars—if indeed you can count them." Then he said to him, "So shall your offspring be." (Genesis 15:2–5)

Descendants as countless as the stars . . . such was the promise made to an old man who had no children and a relatively old wife. I can just think of the tears Sarai must have shed night after night, hearing this promise that God had made to her husband, and yet she couldn't have a baby. Do you think she used to dream about baby names or making clothes and food for her child?

I can relate. It took us years to get pregnant. For years, the doctors said they just didn't know what to tell us to do. We went ahead with IVF, and finally, it happened. I'll never forget receiving that phone call when they called to say that it had worked. When we went for the first ultrasound, I remember the tech turning to me and saying there were two heartbeats. I said, "My baby has two hearts? Can you fix that? What do you mean? . . . There are two babies?!"

Isn't that just like the Lord? Just when I doubted Him, He came through, times two!

I know though that many women beg God for the same miracle who haven't gotten the same answer. My heart immediately breaks for those that are still broken, still hurting and waiting for their miracle.

I wonder how Sarah's arms and Abraham's heart must have ached as they thought about the children they didn't have. Not to mention how they must have felt about God! What a struggle it must have been for them to wait on Him and believe that what was promised actually would happen. That they would not only be parents but the origin of a great race! That must have seemed ludicrous, especially given their age.

I'm reminded of the significance of age for singers. As a vocalist, if you haven't "made it" by your early twenties, you can just about forget a career as a recording artist. Commercially, our world's standards demand youth and beauty and sex appeal. Clearly, our standards are ridiculously and tragically short-sighted.

Truth is, physiologically, your voice doesn't even reach its full maturity in your twenties. Not even in your thirties! Singers reach full vocal maturity around age forty-five. That's when the sound reaches its fullest, most colorful tone.

If all singers were to quit once they passed their prime as dictated by our culture's standards, what a tragedy that would be! We would never hear the human voice at its best, at its richest.

Abraham and Sarah's fullest potential also seemed to be working on a delay. When it came to having kids, they were done. As far as the world was concerned, men his age didn't, and women her age couldn't conceive.

I bet they resigned themselves to being childless and attempted to make peace with it somewhere along the way. It was what they knew. While not preferable, the familiar had oddly become a comfort zone.

That's a sad statement. They convinced themselves that they had no choice but to accept the very thing that broke their hearts—being childless. They assumed they were helpless to change their circumstances and settled.

Even when God spoke to Abraham, promising him an heir, it was unbelievable still to both Abraham and Sarah. Parenthood to even one child had eluded them up to that point. Birthing a nation must have seemed utterly preposterous.

I suppose that was the motivation behind what they did next. Which, as a wife, I find pretty unbelievable.

Somehow they got the idea that they needed to help God out in fulfilling this promise.

> Now Sarai, Abram's wife, had borne him no children. But she had an Egyptian slave named Hagar; so she said to Abram, "The LORD has kept me from having children. Go, sleep with my slave; perhaps I can build a family through her."
>
> Abram agreed to what Sarai said. So after Abram had been living in Canaan ten years, Sarai his wife took her Egyptian slave Hagar and gave her to her husband to be his wife. He slept with Hagar, and she conceived. (Genesis 16:1–4)

Whoever said the Bible was boring must not have been reading very closely. This is intense, the stuff of soap operas! It also reveals the state of their faith up to that point.

Somewhere along the way, they must have at least somewhat bought into the idea that Abraham would father children and beget, beget, beget until he was the originator of a nation greater in numbers than the stars.

Up to that point, the range of their lives—in this case,

relationships, faith, people, prayer, etc.—had been well-defined. This prophecy was new and most certainly beyond their assumed capacity. Sarah didn't believe she could have children, but must have thought God needed some help in the heir-creation process. So she did what anyone would do—told her husband to get another woman pregnant.

Please note my sarcasm. Could you picture yourself actually asking your husband to sleep with another woman? Yeah, that's what I thought.

Unsurprisingly, all did not go swimmingly.

> When she knew she was pregnant, she began to despise her mistress. Then Sarai said to Abram, "You are responsible for the wrong I am suffering. I put my slave in your arms, and now that she knows she is pregnant, she despises me. May the LORD judge between you and me."
>
> "Your slave is in your hands," Abram said. "Do with her whatever you think best." Then Sarai mistreated Hagar; so she fled from her. (Genesis 16:4b–6)

Abraham and Sarah decided they could handle the situation better than God, and ultimately it blew up in their faces. Broken relationships, a son born out of desperation, then shunned for circumstances beyond his control . . .

How heart-breaking! To add insult to injury, dear old Dad abandoned his son, leaving Hagar's and Ishmael's future in the hands of his bitter wife. Ultimately, Hagar was made to leave. She was sent out into the desert with her son, Abraham's son, who nearly died, but for the saving intervention of God.

> God heard the boy crying, and the angel of God called to Hagar from heaven and said to her, "What is

the matter, Hagar? Do not be afraid; God has heard the
boy crying as he lies there. Lift the boy up and take him
by the hand, for I will make him into a great nation."
(Genesis 21:17–18)

Because Abraham and Sarah didn't trust God to follow
through on His end, they forced a situation that ultimately
hurt all the parties involved.

Don't Force It

Vocally, if you try to force yourself to be someone you're
not, there's a very real chance that you could seriously injure
your vocal cords or even lose your voice permanently. When
you try to manipulate God's handiwork, the outcomes are
typically not so great.

For example, let's say that you are great with people one-
on-one. Don't feel badly or less than if you're not teaching a
class or leading worship. Likewise, if you thrive in a professional environment, there's no need to feel guilt or shame if
you don't leave the professional sphere to homeschool.

Abraham and Sarah didn't have the advantage of perspective that we have as we read their story. Unable to step back and
see a bigger picture, both harbored considerable doubts about
God's promise. Even in their unbelief, however, God was relentless in His pursuit of Abraham as the father of many nations.

When Abram was ninety-nine years old, the LORD
appeared to him and said, "I am God Almighty; walk
before me faithfully and be blameless. Then I will make
my covenant between me and you and will greatly increase
your numbers."

Abram fell facedown, and God said to him, "As for me, this is my covenant with you: You will be the father of many nations. No longer will you be called Abram; your name will be Abraham, for I have made you a father of many nations. I will make you very fruitful; I will make nations of you, and kings will come from you. I will establish my covenant as an everlasting covenant between me and you and your descendants after you for the generations to come, to be your God and the God of your descendants after you."

. . . God also said to Abraham . . . "I will bless [your wife] and will surely give you a son by her. I will bless her so that she will be the mother of nations; kings of peoples will come from her."

Abraham fell facedown; he laughed and said to himself, "Will a son be born to a man a hundred years old? Will Sarah bear a child at the age of ninety?" (Genesis 17:1–7, 15–17)

I had my children in my thirties, and surrendering my family planning to God was one of the hardest things I've ever had to do.

I'll never forget the moment I got the call. I was backstage getting ready to perform with Wynonna Judd in Nashville's Ryman auditorium—a lifetime achievement and dream for any music artist—but I wasn't going to ignore a call from my doctor's office. My husband Bernie and I had put off the idea of starting a family for the first five years of marriage, because our careers and travel schedule were so demanding. But we were finally ready. We dreamed about the little boy or girl we couldn't wait to welcome into our family.

"We have your tests back," the nurse said, and I held my

breath. "I'm sorry to tell you this, but the results show you and your husband have less than a 3 percent chance of conceiving a child." I was devastated. I wanted to go home—to hide, to scream and cry—anything but get out there in the spotlight just when I was feeling at my most helpless, my most vulnerable.

But I did. I sang the words "He's gonna bring it all together for good" over and over again. That night I struggled to believe what I was singing. But how I felt in that moment didn't change the truth of what I was singing.

After much prayer and advice from our doctors, Bernie and I decided to pursue fertility treatments. Many tests and shots and doctor's appointments later, the sonogram revealed not one, but two heartbeats! Bella and Gracie became our miracle girls—healthy, beautiful, more than we'd ever asked for.

But God wasn't quite finished with His surprises. Just when our lives were settling back into normalcy, when the twins were three, I discovered there was another miracle baby. This one had come about with no tests, no fertility treatments. And I'll be honest—I hadn't asked for this miracle; we certainly hadn't tried for it, and I was scared. Scared of how this was going to stretch us beyond capacity when our lives were already so full.

Welcome Sadie, our miracle girl number three. She brings us joy in ways we never thought possible. She is more than we'd ever asked for, and that is an incredible gift.

Navigating all of this in my thirties was difficult, especially when I had no idea what God had up His sleeve. I cannot fathom a ninety-year-old woman giving birth. Neither could Abraham. But God wasn't through with Abraham yet.

Not long after the above conversation, Abraham had three visitors, one of whom was the Lord. Abraham asked servants to prepare food. In the meantime, Abraham returned to the tent where the visitors were waiting and the following conversation took place:

> "Where is your wife Sarah?" they asked him.
>
> "There, in the tent," he said.
>
> Then one of them said, "I will surely return to you about this time next year, and Sarah your wife will have a son."
>
> Now Sarah was listening at the entrance to the tent, which was behind him. Abraham and Sarah were already very old, and Sarah was past the age of childbearing. So Sarah laughed to herself as she thought, "After I am worn out and my lord is old, will I now have this pleasure?"
>
> Then the LORD said to Abraham, "Why did Sarah laugh and say, 'Will I really have a child, now that I am old?' Is anything too hard for the LORD? I will return to you at the appointed time next year, and Sarah will have a son."
>
> Sarah was afraid, so she lied and said, "I did not laugh."
>
> But he said, "Yes, you did laugh." (Genesis 18:9–15)

I used to think Sarah was insane for having the audacity to laugh at something the Lord had said . . . and then lie about it. Now, however, I realize that my perspective is one that developed thousands of years after the fact. I know all about Isaac and the nation of Israel. I have an Old Testament and a New Testament full of miraculous signs and events. I've got history on my side.

Sarah had none of that. Here was a post-menopausal woman with a hundred-year-old husband, who had been barren her entire life. Of course, it seems ridiculous to suggest she might have a baby. According to the rules of culture and the physiological limitations that exist in nature, pregnancy is virtually impossible.

Had I been there, I would have probably had a laugh with her.

And had I been caught laughing, I probably would have lied about it too. It must have been terrifying to be called out by God.

Three chapters later, enter the miracle baby.

> Now the LORD was gracious to Sarah as he had said, and the LORD did for Sarah what he had promised. Sarah became pregnant and bore a son to Abraham in his old age, at the very time God had promised him. Abraham gave the name Isaac to the son Sarah bore him. When his son Isaac was eight days old, Abraham circumcised him, as God commanded him. Abraham was a hundred years old when his son Isaac was born to him.
>
> Sarah said, "God has brought me laughter, and everyone who hears about this will laugh with me." And she added, "Who would have said to Abraham that Sarah would nurse children? Yet I have borne him a son in his old age." (Genesis 21:1–7)

I like to think God cracked a smile when this beautiful story came full-circle—from Sarah's laughter over the prospect of a child to a child whose name, Isaac, literally means laughter. Isn't it just like Him to bookend this story with a smile? He didn't berate them for their doubt. He didn't call Sarah out. He gave her joy. He worked His plan exactly as He said He would.

God knew that Abraham and Sarah were going to be the parents of His nation . . . Israel.

He didn't choose them by happenstance. Nor did He choose incorrectly. He knew what the range of Abraham's and Sarah's lives would entail. It just took them a while to catch up.

So what does all of this mean in the real world? In your world?

I'm going to go out on a limb and guess that God has shown or suggested to you what He wants you to do in life. If not, maybe it's because you're not ready to hear it or won't slow down enough to listen.

You were created with a set of skills, personality traits, passions, desires, likes, dislikes. Nothing about you is generic or "done" or past your prime. You are a unique, beautiful, one-of-a-kind creation designed to do unique, beautiful, one-of-a-kind things.

If you've spent your life comparing yourself to others or dreaming that you could be somewhere or someone different, it's time to stop wasting time! Comparisons are dangerous. You'll always find something about yourself that doesn't measure up. And if you dwell on these things, you'll start idolizing and pursuing things other than God and His plan. If your focus is a certain salary, a certain clothing size or a certain pedigree, you're not going to have time or room in your life to consider what God wants from your life.

Sarah's story shows us you can't decide what your range—your thrive zone—is on your terms and pursue God's plan for you at the same time. It's simply not possible.

When that happens, you're missing out on more than you could ever dream for your life. God has created in each of us a distinct and unique tessitura—the sweet spot in which we shine. This range is not on our own terms. We can't force it without straining and causing damage to our heart, our relationships, our voice.

God's "zone" for Sarah, just as it is with us, was far and away better than anything she or we could have come up with. She forced her way to what she wanted, and it turned into a hot mess. But God's tessitura for Sarah turned out to lead to a miracle.

Your range is special and unique. Your thrive zone is where you thrive!

There are specific skills and environments in which you shine. Why run from them?

It's an unfulfilling, exhausting way to live.

Not to mention, in a sense, you're telling God that what He created isn't good enough. You're laughing at His plan. Obviously, our resistance isn't going to throw off God's ultimate plan. His will shall come to pass. Whether you are a part of it is really your decision.

He created you to have a life filled with the joy of knowing Him and knowing that you are fulfilling your true call in life. To run from that, to force something to happen unnaturally, is the making of a really miserable way to live.

FIND WHERE YOU SHINE

Your unique tessitura isn't a concession. It's the acceptance of who you really are. There is power in that. It means you are living and working from a position of strength, which is not only empowering but allows you to have a greater impact on the world around you. It's your thrive zone.

Striving to sing in a range that's not your own or living in a way that's forced is a selfish way to live. Can you image Beyoncé trying to rap like Lecrae? Or Pharrell Williams trying to channel Adele? I just don't see that working. Not only is it just odd, but they would also be short-changing themselves, their unique talent, and their fans.

Similarly, if you're trying to make it in a profession that is not for you or pursue something for the sole purpose of proving that you can do it, that's a selfish way to live. Your intention is to prove that you're better or just as good as someone else. You're basically telling God that you're a little bored with His plan for your life or how He made you, so you're going to do it your way.

It's not a viable way to live.

Even if you manage to pull it off and achieve some success in worldly terms, life is going to feel somewhat hollow and without purpose.

So what do you do?

Do what a good singer does. They sit at a piano and they sing scales and exercises and work their way up and down the keyboard to discover the natural brilliance of their voice—or where the vocal quality diminishes. It's not a glamorous or very fun exercise, but a prudent and helpful one.

Perhaps it's time to sit down with a piece of paper and run up and down the scales that comprise your life. Look at your life. What's working—in your family, your friendships, your daily rhythms, your career, your personal walk with Jesus? What's not working in these areas? When do you feel relaxed and happy? When do you feel uncomfortable? What things seem to always go well? What things seem to always fall apart? Is there a particular role you have aimed for but have come up short time and time again? Is there a profession that you have walked away from despite it being a good fit with your skills and experience?

What's your end game? Are you working to prove something? Or to do something? Are you praying about your life and the scope of it? Are you listening for God's instruction and timing or are you just taking it into your own hands?

These aren't easy questions and certainly aren't meant to make you feel bad about yourself. Quite the opposite, in fact. They're intended to help you assess what in your life is contributing to or impeding your overall happiness and sense of purpose. Stop wasting time trying to be someone you're not.

I have a friend who was in the journalism arena of the music business for years before jumping into the role of a publicist. She wasn't necessarily happy in the new position, but the salary was better and the company more high profile, and it seemed overall like a step up the cultural and corporate ladder.

Soon into her new job, she wrote a bio for one of her artists, a well-known, well-established group. One of the singers told her that she was "a writer pretending to be a publicist."

That singer was right. Not long after, the position was eliminated, and my friend returned to her roots . . . she returned to the arena in which God had created her to shine.

Are you pretending to be something you're not? Are you afraid that if you don't measure up to others that you're worthless? Like Abraham and Sarah, are you impatiently or fearfully standing in the wings, assuming God's promises have passed you by?

It's time to stop bashing your skills and your nature.

God knit you together. He doesn't make mistakes. You are exactly who you are supposed to be. It is now your decision to embrace and live in the fullness of purpose or to run from it.

It's okay if you've slighted your nature in the past. Both Abraham and Sarah laughed in the face of God! It didn't deter His plan or blessing. Nothing you do, think, feel, or say is too much for Him. It is impossible for you to diminish His love for you. Why do you continue to diminish your love for yourself?

Like a singer's voice soaring within their tessitura, when we are living fully within our thrive zones, we begin to operate from the center of our strengths. And we begin to see a fuller picture of the kind of impossible miracles God is capable of.

Chapter 4

TRAINING IN THE WILDERNESS

———— &⁊ ————

Instruct the wise and they will be wiser still;
teach the righteous and they will add to their
learning.

Proverbs 9:9

*M*ost professional voice coaches recommend not to start
vocal training until age thirteen or fourteen. The voice
is a product of working the right muscles that develop and
mature right along with the rest of the body. For most classi-
cally trained singers, instruction begins in their early teens and
picks up intensity when they go to college or a conservatory.
After that, it wouldn't be unusual to pursue post-graduate
training before joining a company or other professional singing organization.

Commercial singers—the smart ones—will also often
continue training throughout their career. Training keeps
the muscles in shape, the technique polished and, hopefully,
extends the longevity of a healthy voice.

If ever there were an advocate for education, it was Jesus.
His entire ministry focused on teaching . . . through parables,
exposition, miracles, preaching. He never sifted through a
crowd to find those who seemed to be further behind in life

and zero in on their deficiencies. He never indicated that even a pillar of society would not benefit from what He had to say. He understood that humanity—with the capacity to retain new information, process new ideas, and live a life that gets better and better with each new day and each discovery—is constantly developing and learning.

We can glean an endless amount of inspiration and encouragement from Jesus as teacher. But in those moments when Jesus Himself was being refined, He becomes a living example of how we should train our hearts, souls, and minds for our callings.

His forty days in the wilderness (Matthew 4:1–11) provide a model of pretraining commitment and preparation, focus, goal-setting, and follow-through. Moreover, Jesus' three tests supply universal, foundational lessons on which to build the profession of your choice and a passion out of your calling. We'll get into His responses more in a bit, but for now, here's a preview:

1. "Man shall not live on bread alone" (Matthew 4:4). Don't define success or orient your life around material gain.
2. "Do not put the Lord your God to the test" (4:7). Don't live your life recklessly and expect God to be the one to save you. You have to do the work.
3. "Worship the Lord your God, and serve him only" (4:10). Whatever your priorities are in life—work, family, church, reputation, money—if any of it pushes God out of the top position, you're headed for a train wreck.

I would be better off losing my voice forever than losing my faith, which is my priority and my solid foundation. As you are on the path to discovering your true passion, you can't compromise your belief system for anything or anyone. You absolutely must establish your convictions before you get out there in this chaotic and often manipulative world. You will inevitably face challenges, defeats, and temptations along the way. You won't be equipped to confront and rise above them if you don't put in the work and solidify your faith beforehand.

I'm convinced that, like most things He did in His human life, Jesus did not submit to this testing in the desert for His sake. His baptism wasn't for His own sins. As part of the triumvirate, He is part of the Three-in-One Trinity. He's in!

When Christ entered this world as a baby, He made Himself not just our Savior; He became one of us. He faced the same trials that everyone faces. He had to rise above the same temptations that we all do. His triumph over sin and temptation wasn't simply to boost His reputation; it was to teach us how to navigate the treacherous waters around us. If we could or would take the time to absorb fully the lessons of His life, ours would never be the same.

YOU HAVE TO START SOMEWHERE

*T*here's quite a bit to be said about Jesus' life leading up to the beginning of His ministry at age thirty. One time, when He was just a preteen, Jesus went missing. After frantic searching, Mary and Joseph found their young son learning from and conversing with the leaders of the Temple.

Remember that exchange?

> After three days they found him in the temple courts, sitting among the teachers, listening to them and asking them questions. Everyone who heard him was amazed

at his understanding and his answers. When his parents saw him, they were astonished. His mother said to him, "Son, why have you treated us like this? Your father and I have been anxiously searching for you." (Luke 2:46–48)

They said that so much more delicately than I would have. Three days feels like an eternity to be without your child—especially a twelve-year-old. I would be in hysterics at that point. And I might have come unglued at his response . . . "'Why were you searching for me?' he asked. 'Didn't you know I had to be in my Father's house?' But they did not understand what he was saying to them" (Luke 2:49–50).

Again, not sure how well I would have handled that. I would definitely have taken some offense to my child insisting on being away from home. But I think it's obvious that Jesus' response had nothing to do with appeasing His stressed-out parents. It was a teaching moment. He said He had to be in His Father's House. That tells me that being in the Father's House, or in current vernacular, church, is important. Not just important—essential. At twelve years of age, Jesus was already demonstrating godly priorities, which He continued to do, as stated in the next two verses.

"Then he went down to Nazareth with them and was obedient to them. But his mother treasured all these things in her heart. And Jesus grew in wisdom and stature, and in favor with God and man" (Luke 2:51–52). These two verses are such beautiful representations of His humanity. He was a child who had to obey His parents. As He grew up (stature), He learned things (wisdom). In other words, He wasn't born a super-baby. He was born to develop and grow just like the rest of us. While we don't see any examples of Jesus in adolescence, there are certain indicators that He lived just like everybody else.

For example, we know that He was a carpenter. During the period of time in which He lived, most tradesmen began their training in childhood. I like to picture Joseph teaching his Son how to use a hammer or wield a blade. The King of Kings probably grew up with sawdust in His hair and blisters on His hands.

Also, the story of His disappearance to the temple indicates that Jesus was not afraid of people but sought them out at an early age. Later in life, we see His commitment to building solid relationships within His recruitment of and ministry with the twelve disciples. The favor He bestowed upon social outcasts—lepers, tax collectors, prostitutes—is indicative of His compassionate heart and embracing nature. He loved God and people and made an effort to be in positive relationship with both.

Whereas many of us in today's world tend to compartmentalize our spiritual lives, professional lives, social lives, etc., we can see pretty clearly that that is not the example Jesus set. His lifestyle was such that, in the verses above, Luke aligns Jesus' relationship with God and man within the same phrase. It's a powerful example and compelling thought, particularly for those of us who do not have jobs in a traditional "ministry" or "Christian" organization or business.

Do you have different behaviors or guidelines when you're not with a typical church crowd? Is your professional lifestyle a departure from the way you behave at a church event or service? If the answer is "yes," you're probably typical. And honestly, it may be difficult to judge which set of behaviors is better. You may be following some different rules while at a church event, but are you authentic? While you're at work, you may feel more like yourself, but are your behaviors or interactions with other people ones that honor God?

It's worth remembering that God doesn't just see you when you're at church. He's omniscient and omnipresent, meaning He knows all and sees all. That shouldn't scare you. In fact, that should be a comfort to you. Nothing you do can shock or surprise God. If there is any place that you should feel completely safe with all of your scars and mistakes and anger and hurt and joy and celebration, it should be at His feet. He can handle it all, and NOTHING you can do will diminish His love for you.

GOING PUBLIC

O f all of the gospels, Luke's, by far, contains more detail about the early life of Jesus between birth and baptism. Though even that account is pretty vague on the details. There's a gap between chapter 2, when boy Jesus goes home, being obedient and growing in favor, and chapter 3, which picks up with John the Baptist preparing the way for Jesus' ministry. I'm not going to speculate on what's not there; instead, let's look at what is.

In Luke, we see Jesus again at His baptism. Matthew spans a similar frame of time, featuring Jesus again at His baptism. Mark doesn't begin Jesus' story until His baptism. So clearly, baptism is significant.

I think for all of us, whatever our calling may be, Jesus made it clear that a public profession of faith was essential. So essential it should be done first. Before He went into the wilderness, before He performed a miracle, before He taught on a mountainside, Jesus was baptized. He publicly declared whose He was and what He was all about.

This point really can't be overstated. Until you know

Christ, accept Him as your Savior and publicly declare what you believe, you really shouldn't start working on anything else. There's an order here for a reason. Making His faith known was intentional. He was modeling for us the necessity of a public declaration of faith, indicating that it is a key component of a life lived on mission. If your salvation and the dedication of your life to Christ and the acceptance of His blood as redemption for your sins is in question, forget about your passion . . . and let's look at His.

The word passion arises from the Latin word *pati*, which means "to suffer." When we refer to the Passion of the Christ, we refer to His suffering and death on the cross, which was the reason He came to earth at all.

Growing up in a Christian home, I learned what was called the Roman Road when I was a child. It's a series of verses from the book of Romans that describes the human condition (fallen), the consequences of such a state (eternal condemnation), and the one and only way to avoid such a fate (faith in Jesus Christ and His death and resurrection). Looking back at it today, it still resonates with me and the fundamentals to which I've always subscribed. For an adult considering it for the first time, though, I could see how it may seem a bit confusing, if not off-putting.

I think the hardest thing to wrap our heads around is that despite how good we may be—how good anyone may be—without accepting the gift of Christ, we are not saved and thus are not headed for eternity in heaven, which means an eternity in hell.

Many may feel that sounds incredibly harsh, but think about it this way. God created the world and everything in it. But while He is perfect and can have nothing to do with sin, He created us with free will. He didn't force us to be His.

Because of that free will, I think we could all agree that humanity has made some less than stellar decisions throughout the years. When you look around, there is truly something fundamentally wrong with the world. At the heart of that is sin.

Unfortunately, we've all sinned. Romans 3:23 lays that out pretty clearly. "For all have sinned and fall short of the glory of God."

Again, unfortunately, the consequences of sin are steep. "For the wages of sin is death, but the gift of God is eternal life in Christ Jesus our Lord" (Romans 6:23).

Because sin is so bad, a sacrifice was required to cover the sins of man, bringing him back in communion with God. Here's the good news: Jesus' death on the cross was that sacrifice. "But God demonstrates his own love for us in this: While we were still sinners, Christ died for us" (Romans 5:8).

In order to receive that sacrifice, you just have to believe. "If you declare with your mouth, 'Jesus is Lord,' and believe in your heart that God raised him from the dead, you will be saved" (Romans 10:9).

Without my faith and salvation, I would not be alive today. Some of the things I've gone through in life would have taken me out but for that solid foundation. I would be dishonoring you and my own calling if I didn't emphasize how essential the acceptance of Christ is. Your heart influences everything in your world and your eternal destination. It is your anchor, and until it's set, you're going to waver. I am fragile and fragmented, and I can be insensitive and mean and judgmental just as easily as I can be kind and sweet and fun. It is Christ within me that has allowed me to keep my head above the choppiest of waters that otherwise would have taken me under. With Jesus Christ in my life, I stand securely.

One of the most beautiful moments in history, as recorded in Scripture, is Jesus coming out of the water following His baptism:

> When all the people were being baptized, Jesus was baptized too. And as he was praying, heaven was opened and the Holy Spirit descended on him in bodily form like a dove. And a voice came from heaven: "You are my Son, whom I love; with you I am well pleased." (Luke 3:21–22)

Talk about a green light commissioning you to embark upon your life's work! It makes me think of a graduation. You've walked the stage, you're holding your diploma, and then you toss that hat in the air. *Welcome to the world! . . .* Well, not quite; as you likely know, the education continues after graduation, when you are required to put your training to work.

Jesus had the training. He had made a public profession and was met with God's approval. But before Jesus could begin His ministry, He'd have to pass some serious, real-world tests.

OFF TO THE WILDERNESS

> Jesus, full of the Holy Spirit, left the Jordan and was led by the Spirit into the wilderness. (Luke 4:1)

> Then Jesus was led by the Spirit into the wilderness to be tempted by the devil. (Matthew 4:1)

> At once the Spirit sent him out into the wilderness, and he was in the wilderness forty days, being tempted

by Satan. He was with the wild animals, and angels attended him. (Mark 1:12–13)

Notice the role the Spirit plays here. Towards the end of His life, Jesus said He would send a Helper, the Holy Spirit. "But the Advocate, the Holy Spirit, whom the Father will send in my name, will teach you all things and will remind you of everything I have said to you" (John 14:26).

The Helper is here. We have full access to guidance and wisdom. Much like the Spirit led Jesus to the wilderness—to the training ground—the Spirit will lead us to our own arena of trial, testing, and preparation among the "wild animals"— bosses, doctors, colleagues, boyfriends, lawyers, contractors, relatives, [*fill in the blank*] . . .

Our world is hard, so many people don armor and build up walls just trying to survive. These barriers make relationships and progress difficult. When we allow ourselves to be led by the Spirit instead of self-interest, we should expect that the journey won't be safe, but it will not be one we have to face alone.

Lighting the Match

Pain and anguish that can make or break you: *This is trial by fire.*

The wilderness trials didn't get rolling until Jesus had been fasting for forty days. Gandhi only fasted for twenty-one days! Can you imagine the physical state one would be in after forty? It seems like His fast was the match that sparked the fire. Jesus was weak. Satan bided His time and swooped in strategically and relentlessly. To fully appreciate that entire span of time, I find it much more impactful and insightful to look at the "training session" as a whole. Let's watch it unfold in Luke 4.

> Jesus, full of the Holy Spirit, left the Jordan and was led by the Spirit into the wilderness, where for forty days he was tempted by the devil. He ate nothing during those days, and at the end of them he was hungry.
>
> The devil said to him, "If you are the Son of God, tell this stone to become bread."
>
> Jesus answered, "It is written: 'Man shall not live on bread alone.'" (vv. 1–3)

Do you remember the last time you skipped a meal or several? Did you feel weak, faint, "hangry" (hungry and angry)? Because Jesus was fully man, while also fully God, His body was fully affected by the physical realities that plague the rest of us. He was starving, and Satan tried to exploit His physical condition. Even as His stomach was rumbling, however, His voice was firm. Jesus' response affirms that even when we are weak, His strength is made perfect within us.

> The devil led him up to a high place and showed him in an instant all the kingdoms of the world. And he said to him, "I will give you all their authority and splendor; it has been given to me, and I can give it to anyone I want to. If you worship me, it will all be yours."
>
> Jesus answered, "It is written: 'Worship the Lord your God and serve him only.'" (Luke 4:5–8)

Strike two.

When is the last time you got a promotion? Or jumped up a pay grade? Feels good, right? Again, appealing to Jesus' humanity, Satan offers the son of a carpenter power and the riches of the world that accompany it. Once again, Jesus deflects the temptation not by pointing out the strength of

His own character or resolve, but by shifting the focus back to God.

> The devil led him to Jerusalem and had him stand on the highest point of the temple. "If you are the Son of God," he said, "throw yourself down from here. For it is written:
> "'He will command his angels concerning you
> to guard you carefully;
> they will lift you up in their hands,
> so that you will not strike your foot against a stone.'"
> Jesus answered, "It is said: 'Do not put the Lord your God to the test.'"
> When the devil had finished all this tempting, he left him until an opportune time. (vv. 9–13)

Jesus reacts to this final temptation in a manner definitive enough to send Satan on his way, completing the triad of temptations that pull on us so frequently—sustenance, power, and pride. These things motivate us, challenge us and change us, for better or worse.

By giving the pursuit of those things—sustenance, power, pride—so much weight in our lives, we make ourselves vulnerable to compromise. It becomes easy to stray from moral absolutes, to justify cutting corners or to put down others in an attempt to boost our reputations. Temptation is a slippery slope, inching further away from truth. Without truth, we lose our conviction of who God is and the role we should allow Him to play in our lives. Our false pride in our own strength and ability to handle everything life throws at us can create blind spots. We can lose our way without even realizing it.

If we hope to avoid this dangerous decline, we have to

shore up our grit, determination, and beliefs. We have to be even more strategic than the one tempting us. And we need to have that strategy mapped out before the tests begin. Just like Jesus did.

Stand Your Ground

Keep in mind, during the wilderness temptations, Jesus still hasn't eaten. He's still weak and exhausted. But here, Jesus shows us that even in hunger and fatigue, it's possible to stand your ground and stay true to who you are. He employs a winning strategy and never waivers.

His defense is the Word of God.

And His responses are as relevant today as they were then.

Jesus answered, "It is written: 'Man shall not live on bread alone'" (Luke 4:4).

Priorities 101 right there. Your profession or lifestyle should never be predicted by what you hope to gain in personal reward. Not to say that providing a living for yourself and your family isn't important. You have to put food on the table, and prosperity or material blessing are not wrong in and of themselves. However, if our primary motivation in life is monetary or material gain, we're setting ourselves up for disaster. Notice, Jesus does not say that bread isn't important. He just says it's not the only thing we depend on to sustain life.

As you reflect on your life choices and pursuits, what has been your motivation? Many of us compromise what we really want to do for a better salary. We choose to be who we think we should be instead of who we are, only to find out, usually painfully, that you truly can't buy happiness, passion, or purpose.

Very often, I hear pastors or Sunday School teachers or

worship leaders use the phrase "seek God's face." It's a beautiful construct and makes for a great song lyric, but "seeking His face" can easily become hollow Christianese if not accompanied by physical action. How do you seek His face? Where do you look? The answer will be different for everyone as God reveals Himself in mysterious, personal ways, but there's one foolproof place to start—Scripture.

The Bible contains hundreds of lessons about material gain and financial responsibility. It illustrates what being a good steward is all about (Matthew 25:14–30). It looks at the role money should play in relationships—with other people, with the church, even with the government.

Somehow I doubt that God's intent here was to turn us all into financial planners or wealth advisors. Rather, He gave us these rules and guidelines about money so we could live a life free of worrying about money! If you're a good steward, financially responsible and self-sufficient, you won't be forced into taking a certain job because you need the money. Likewise, if you can truly let go of the world's perspective on money and embrace God's perspective, you will break through countless chains that have likely weighed you down for most of your life.

Suddenly, instead of hating the neighbors because of the new addition they're putting on their house to accommodate a new boat or new car . . . you can just be neighbors.

God can change your heart that radically. He did, after all, convince twelve grown men to ditch their jobs, their salaries, and their reputations to serve Him as disciples without twisting their arms. He simply revealed the truth and beauty of who He was and why He was there. It was such a captivating presentation, their life goals changed immediately. Jesus and His love and His Heavenly Father became the prize. Eternal life trumped livelihood.

Jesus answered, "It is written: 'Worship the Lord your God and serve him only'" (Luke 4:8).

I think it would be so much easier to avoid idol worship if there were actual gold idols and figurines that we knew to steer clear of. While these do exist, the idols to which we tend to succumb are much more subtle. Many times we don't even recognize one that's right before our eyes, nor would we ever label ourselves as idolaters.

But when you look at the definition—something or someone that you revere, worship, or admire apart from God—most people could start ticking off names of people and things that easily fit the bill.

That's not to say that everything or everyone you admire is an idol. Only those things or people that you revere or worship more than God are idols.

You can usually determine where things stack up in your heart and mind by evaluating where you spend your time and money. When you've identified those investments, answer this question: "Why? Why is this something I prioritize, and to what end?"

When Satan tempted Jesus, he led with a grand proposal of all that he would give Jesus. Kingdoms, wealth, power . . . the whole world if Jesus would just bow down.

He was essentially bribing Jesus.

Modern culture works the same way. Everything seems to be based on "What can you do for me?" or "What will you give me if I do this for you?" That's conditional thinking. Our God is unconditional. He is God not because of what He does or gives. He is God because of who He is.

I don't recall Jesus giving handouts or promising wealth and power. In the Scriptures, Jesus loved on people. When He talked about God, He didn't mention His wealth. He spoke of His love.

Another significant distinction and something to keep in mind when you think of your focus and priorities in life . . . Every "god" or idol other than God is temporal. Their rewards are temporal. Their reigns are temporal. Only God is eternal. God's Kingdom is not here. Therefore, those who follow Him and Him alone are free not to be shackled down by this world.

As you think about your voice, your passion, your role in this world, start thinking about your ultimate ambition. If your goals begin and end on this earth, you're probably establishing some idols in your life. If your job and people you hang out with are primarily means of financial gain, sexual satisfaction, or reputation, your end game is conditional; and your goals, conquests, achievements could easily become idols if they're not already.

And listen, you can live your God-given passions and talents out loud in a multitude of ways. Many people believe the lie that you can only "really" serve God through full-time ministry. While ministry is commendable and valuable, it is not the only way!

Take a step back and think about who you are and the kind of life you want to lead. If you're an accountant, how can you use your position to show God's love to someone? If you're a nurse or banker or a publicist or a teacher, what are you doing to let people see God in you each day? If you are a minister, how can you continue to shift the focus and glory to God, not on you? Do you genuinely care about the people who come in and out of your daily life? Do you think about them as part of God's design?

At the end of the day, be honest with yourself. What do you want? Who do you want? And why?

You have to know your God before you can ever know who you are.

Jesus answered, "It is said: 'Do not put the Lord your God to the test'" (Luke 4:12).

God made the heavens and the earth and man and woman and every creature. Jesus spent a lot of His time among us performing miracles. As we look further, we see water turned to wine, lepers healed, the blind receiving their sight, the lame walking, even the dead rising. Our God can do anything. When Satan told Jesus to jump from a cliff to let the angels save Him, He could have and He would have been fine. But God's not about using miracles for entertainment value. He's not an act. He's a God who works miracles that save lives, for the short and long term.

It's tempting, at times, to think of God as an ATM for miracles or stuff that we want. Our prayer time can turn into a honey-do list and very quickly, we forget that the point of Christianity and salvation and redemption is a relationship between God and us. Sadly, we often treat our faith like a transaction.

Personally, I can remember when I've issued ultimatums to God! "If you do this or don't do this, I'll stop [a certain negative behavior]."

Or "If you get me through this alive or intact, etc. . . . . I'm yours forever."

I think of the very common scene in almost every war movie or survival documentary. People are at death's door, and that desperate prayer gets tossed out like a lifeline: "God, if you get me through this alive . . ."

We are so arrogant at times, believing God is at our disposal. We demonstrate such a lack of humility and respect when we cry out for whatever it is we think we need. Especially when we haven't bothered to talk with Him consistently.

God isn't life insurance. It was never His plan or intent

for us to do whatever it is we want and He'll catch us like a safety net. He gave us free will, so we live in a fallen world as fallen people without any promises that our actions would be immune to consequence. If we stand on the edge of a cliff and yell out, "God if you save me from this, I'm yours forever," and jump, we still fall off a cliff.

The whole point here is your paradigm. Living your life thinking God is there to fix things or prevent things creates a very unfortunate environment of expectation. If that's your perspective, and you think that life, God or other people owe you something for whatever reason, your life will be full of disappointment, frustration, and bitterness.

On the other hand, if you perceive your relationship with God as that—a true relationship—you're setting yourself up for a life full of hope. It may not be a life full of happiness, because you're still living it on earth with other people. Things are going to happen that will break your spirit and crush your soul and make you cry yourself to sleep sometimes. But when you face those impending, inevitable heartbreaks with your heart and arm linked with God's, you have not only a constant companion but an eternal advocate who can't wait to spend forever with you. He loves you so much. You are so much more than a to-do list to Him. Take the time to make sure He is more than a checklist or shopping list or wish list to you.

Our God is the God of miracles, and He can do whatever He wants whenever He wants however He wants. It is not your role to demand that He perform. It is your role to love Him, be with Him, and live a life letting Him love you. He does not get you out of messes you've made but loves you through them and helps you put the pieces back together on the other side.

Jesus lived a brief life on this earth, but in His estimated thirty-three years, He lived an exemplary life that was intended to be replicated as closely as possible. He gave us a roadmap to navigate, showing us how to learn and how to love and how to trust. Once we grasp those concepts and apply them with a continually growing knowledge of His word, we're ready to go anywhere, knock on any door, face any obstacle, weather any storm—and find our voice.

Chapter 5

CARING FOR YOUR INSTRUMENT
FROM THE INSIDE OUT

———— ✌ ————

Super Bowl XXV saw the New York Giants take down the Buffalo Bills by a score of 20–19. It is the only Super Bowl decided by one point.

But there was something else noteworthy that happened at that 1991 Championship game. Before the clock began to count down and the players were on the field, Whitney Houston delivered what has been generally agreed upon as the best rendition of "The Star Spangled Banner" ever.

It was a flawless delivery, a pinnacle moment in the career of one of the greatest singers of all time.

In 2012, she was found lifeless in a Los Angeles hotel.

She was forty-eight.

The world felt her staggering loss.

For years, Houston had been on the decline. Her toxic marriage coincided with her descent into drug abuse.

In the years leading up to her death, it was easy to see the damage her body had suffered. Thin and frail, she was a shadow of who she had been. Her voice—that magical, powerful, golden voice—was all but gone.

It was an extreme example of negligence and abuse of an

instrument. Unlike guitar players or drummers or any other musician who can control the quality of their instrument with their wallet or a good tech team, a vocalist's instrument is his or her body. The quality of that instrument resides in the quality of care each singer provides for themselves.

The voice of all voices wasn't immune to poor care. As Whitney destroyed her body with drugs, poor nutrition, and an all-around dangerous lifestyle, her voice went down with the ship.

It's also important to point out that in Whitney's case, for example, it wasn't an instance of someone being willfully negligent with their health. It was someone whose mental well-being was in shambles. As her mental health declined, her body and voice paid the price.

Every singer's success and longevity hinge on his or her well-being. Not too long ago, though, my own well-being was at risk. Postpartum depression was dragging me down. Not only could I not enjoy life, I wasn't healthy. My nutrition was off, my sleep routine was off . . . my voice was off. I could hear a marked difference in my voice on those days when I was taking care of myself and those days I wasn't.

On top of all of this, I felt the constant pressure from media and society to look a certain way—a standard complicated by the inevitable baby weight I carried after the birth of my third daughter. Particularly in the entertainment industry, your appearance is deemed imperative to your success. The pressure to be a certain size and to look no older than a certain age is often insurmountable, and it takes a lot of entertainers—especially women—down a dangerous spiral that compromises not only their careers but their overall quality of life.

All of this is cyclical. As a singer, if you're taking care of your body, your voice will be stronger. If your voice is stronger, your success will be greater. The greater your success, the more confidence you'll feel and exhibit, which will directly impact your relationships with God, with others, and with yourself. The same is true of any calling; physical vitality has significant bearing on emotions, connections and passions, and vice versa.

Say you're in a troubled relationship and your coping mechanism—be it alcohol, drugs, food, or other—compromises your self-care. Your body—your instrument, and your voice—will reflect that. If it declines, your success will too. It's inevitable.

The solution seems obvious—eat right, sleep well, honor your body, and good things will follow. For women, however, that plan requires some caution. So many of us hesitate to focus on self-care out of guilt, shame, or lack of time. The world expects superwomen: devoted wives, fun and caring moms, driven professionals, community volunteers, church leaders, family managers—all the while effortlessly being thin and beautiful. Need I go on?

There is so much pressure for us to master everything, and many of us—myself included—chronically try to please everyone. We'll sacrifice our health and well-being to meet expectations—an ironically self-centered perspective, given that it involves neglecting our best interests. Soon we're in that downward cycle. We'd like to think that, even when we're struggling, the effects aren't felt by others; but somewhere inside, we all know that's not true.

When I'm down mentally or physically, I'm not the mom and wife I want to be. If I'm singularly focused on meeting every expectation, my head becomes consumed with me, me, and more of me. My heart and my music become never-ending projects; I can never quite get things together enough to share them. My lack of confidence causes me to withdraw, and before long, my world becomes very small. I rob my children, my husband, my friends, and my fans of the opportunity to do life in fellowship with me.

When Whitney Houston died, the world was robbed of one of the greatest talents of all time. The same could be said in the case of performers like Janis Joplin, Heath Ledger, Michael Jackson, Philip Seymour Hoffman, Amy Winehouse, Robin Williams . . . and sadly, the list goes on. These people were masters of their craft. They had fans all over the world. Yet their talent wasn't enough to pull them out of the darkness they had lived in for too long. When they were gone, their family, their friends, the world missed out on all they had to offer.

But for our own lives, we can hold fast to the truth that Scripture tells us to treat our bodies as living temples. God did not design our bodies for any kind of abuse—whether drugs or alcohol abuse, starving ourselves or overeating, or going for dangerous stretches of time without sleep. We will never realize our full potential in any area if we're sick or weak or addicted. God has great work for all of us but needs us to be healthy, strong, and mentally prepared to go out in the field.

There are many practical things you can do to step towards good health. At times, there seems to be a chicken or egg scenario going on. Does good physical health lead to good mental health? Or does good mental health lead to good physical health? Personally, I think the answer is yes. They both contribute to each other—so you have to care intently for both.

I learned this the hard way.

I remember the day it all started. I was in college. My boyfriend was that guy all the girls had crushes on. He cruised around campus in his flashy red car, and somehow, he had picked me. And I was desperate to keep him happy. One day we were at the grocery store, and he pointed out a girl on a magazine cover.

"Do you see this? She's perfect. *That's* what I think is beautiful."

I remember thinking, *But I'll never look like that. Not with all the surgeries in the world.*

That afternoon, we went to lunch, after which I excused myself and went to the bathroom. That was the first time I ever made myself throw up.

I grew up with two godly parents who loved me and believed in me and built me up, yet I had still struggled with my self-image throughout my teen years. But this was the day it kicked into overdrive. After lunch that day, I made a decision.

I remember going to the restaurant's bathroom, locking the door, and getting down on my knees. I was crying, but I was determined. I remember shoving my fingers down my throat, and when I did, it was like opening Pandora's box. Once I started, I felt I couldn't stop. Every day, I locked myself in the bathroom and continued my purging habit. Every day, I hoped it would be enough to keep my boyfriend around.

My teeth began to turn yellow. My ribs began to stick out through my shirt. My hair began to fall out as I withheld the nutrients my body needed. My boyfriend—who, unfortunately, soon became my fiancé—even paid for me to get braces because he wanted my smile to be perfect. It was a toxic relationship. I did everything out of fear to please him. Meanwhile, I was losing myself.

When you fall into something as deep as bulimia, it takes a lot to get out of it. My family lovingly intervened when they saw I had a problem. God got my attention one day while I was kneeling at the toilet, as I felt His Spirit speak gently, "My grace is enough. My grace is enough." And my doctor told me that if I kept throwing up on purpose, I would ruin my voice.

All these wise voices in my life told me it wasn't worth it. But it took time for me to actually listen and start to change.

I was singing in church at the time, and this touring singing group called Truth came and performed a concert one night. I watched them and thought, *I want to do that. I want to use my voice to sing God's truth.* I realized this was my gift, and it was my purpose. And then I realized something else: my fiancé did not fit with God's plan for my life. He was so controlling, he wouldn't even go to church when I was singing because he didn't approve of me being on stage. He thought my beauty should be just for him.

So I dumped him. I auditioned for Truth, and then I traveled with them for two years—two years in which God began to take the truth of His Word and imprint it on my heart and mind in a transformative way.

I wish I could say I never struggled with my eating disorder again. But my healing has been a long journey. Though I no longer struggle with bulimia, I will struggle with self-image for the rest of my life. But every day, God's grace *is* enough. And every day, I grow closer to Him as I lean on Him to help me live this out.

I had to lean on Him particularly after the birth of my daughter Sadie. Depression was laying claim to my life; I didn't even realize how my relationship with food was dragging me down. This time, I was eating in excess—eating as a way to comfort myself—a pitfall as unhealthy and self-destructive as bulimia had been.

When I finally decided enough was enough and resolved to do something about it, I started by looking at my diet. I cut out refined sugar and processed foods, and I followed a workout plan, but the foundation of all of this was a commitment to start caring for my body. I had to learn how to do that again.

When I was bulimic, I was trying to lose weight to please my fiancé. But this time, I had to focus on losing weight for the sake of being healthy.

I dropped forty pounds. I felt better than I had in years.

For me, though, the real victory wasn't the weight loss. It wasn't about reaching a certain size of figure. The real victory was in learning to take care of my whole temple—the inner and outer me.

It's the airplane oxygen-mask scenario. Adults are to put the mask on themselves before their children. Why? If they pass out, their kids are out of luck. If I diminish my health, I am no good to anyone else.

The great news about all of this is that it's never too late! You can always do something to make your mind and body healthier. Even if you've tried and failed to make healthy changes in the past, as Scripture says, mercies are new every morning. You are worth a second or third chance—or however many tries it takes to be healthy. Just like a singer or an athlete, your body is your instrument, your tool. It deserves to be cared for. Fight for your physical health; your mind, heart, relationships, and talent will reap immense rewards.

Bear in mind that even those with the most stalwart resolve are going to make mistakes and have slip-ups from time-to-time, either in neglecting or indulging their needs. It's not a matter of if; it's a matter of when. When it happens, go easy on yourself. You're only human. One bad day doesn't negate the great day before, nor exclude you from the great day to come.

Last thing to keep in mind: Whatever wellness journey you embark on, don't go it alone. I strongly believe you should start and end your days in conversation with the Lord. I also believe that He strategically places certain people in your life to be a help, encouragement, and support. Take advantage of the blessing of relationships.

HEALTHY LIVING 101

Food and Drink

One of my favorite stories in Scripture follows Israel's exile to Babylon when the king recruits the fittest, most handsome men to be trained in his palace and share food and wine of the royal table. Daniel and his friends Shadrach, Meshach, and Abednego weren't buying into the dietary plan. Daniel asked the official overseeing them for an exception to be made so that he and his friends could consume vegetables and water instead. I love what happens next . . .

> Now God had caused the official to show favor and compassion to Daniel, but the official told Daniel, "I am afraid of my lord the king, who has assigned your food and drink. Why should he see you looking worse than the other young men your age? The king would then have my head because of you."
>
> Daniel then said to the guard whom the chief official had appointed over Daniel, Hananiah, Mishael and Azariah, "Please test your servants for ten days: Give us nothing but vegetables to eat and water to drink. Then compare our appearance with that of the young men who eat the royal food, and treat your servants in accordance with what you see." So he agreed to this and tested them for ten days.
>
> At the end of the ten days they looked healthier and

better nourished than any of the young men who ate the royal food. So the guard took away their choice food and the wine they were to drink and gave them vegetables instead." (Daniel 1:9–16)

I think there's so much to be learned here. First, it's pretty clear that a diet consisting of veggies and water is probably going to be more beneficial across the board than one steeped in wine. But beyond the menu, I think the way that this "test" is formatted is a brilliant model for anyone.

So let's start with you! Maybe you have tried every diet and fad and plan under the sun to lose weight, get your blood sugar in check, or keep your cholesterol down, and nothing has worked because you haven't been able to stick to it. Start smaller and give yourself a very finite window of time.

Daniel asked for ten days. That's not a lot of time. But it's enough to see some changes. My guess is that in the past you've gone really extreme for a day or two, noticed no physical changes, felt terrible and gave up. I'm guessing, because I've done the same thing. We live in an instant-gratification world that tells us if we do some crunches, we should immediately expect to see a six-pack. If only it were that easy!

Healthy change is gradual change that can become fully integrated into your life. Drastic change strains your body and your mind. It's hard to implement and even more challenging to sustain.

But when it comes to your health, enough is enough! If you don't have a healthy body, a music career isn't the only thing you'll be missing out on. You can't be the type of parent, partner, friend, employee, employer, or follower of Christ that you want to be if you have no energy and are in and out of the doctor's office all the time.

As we covered earlier, your brain won't function optimally if your nutrition is off. Personally, my brain needs all the help it can get. I'm only sabotaging myself and my potential if I'm denying my body the things that it needs.

I have found that the same dietary guidelines for singers translate really well to just about everyone else. Why? The body is a singer's instrument. For everyone else, the body is still a tool for engaging the rest of the world. I would never expect to be at my best vocally if my diet was out of whack. Why should I expect to be at my best at anything else if I'm not being mindful of what I'm putting into my body?

I'm not recommending that you have to become a vegan or go on some extreme diet. I'm suggesting that for the next ten days, you use your common sense.

Omit the fried, processed foods.

In the morning, opt for cereal and milk over the donut and frappe. Or better yet, include some protein and good fats such as a sandwich with egg and avocado to keep hunger at bay.

At lunch, take a turkey sandwich or grab a salad instead of the burger and fries.

At night, try a grilled or baked protein: chicken, fish, or lean red meat. Add some veggies, a baked potato and a salad.

If you need some snacks or treats during the day, go for fruit or cut vegetables. If you have to have chocolate, have one piece of high-quality dark chocolate or count out five M&Ms.

And when it comes to beverages, I can't say it enough—water, water, water. For a vocalist, you'll never make it far without water. Even if you're not a singer, I think you'll be shocked by the difference in your appearance, energy, and overall health by opting for water over sodas, coffee, wine, etc. You don't have to go cold turkey on other beverage options, but be mindful of the calories, caffeine, and other unnecessary elements you're putting into your body with each cup of . . . whatever.

If all of this sounds boring or tedious, remember . . . ten days! You can do anything for ten days. And at the end of those ten days, see how you feel. See how you look, how you sleep, how your clothes are fitting.

The goal here is twofold. First and foremost, you want to optimize your health. A wholesome diet will do that for anyone of any size with any condition. Beyond that, another huge goal is to begin separating food from your emotional life. Many women might observe diet patterns related to their emotions. Happy or sad, celebrating or mourning, burning the midnight oil or trying to make everyone around us happy, mood swings are often accompanied by skipped meals or intense cravings.

It's time to disassociate your diet with your feelings. Not to say that meal time shouldn't be enjoyable or you should stop entering social situations that involve food. Rather, for ten days, reframe the role of food in your life. Make it your fuel—not your crutch. Once you do that, you're removing the power that food has over you and your well-being.

If it's too difficult for you to make those changes on your own, visit a nutritionist. Talk with your doctor. Make a plan. Let yourself take care of . . . yourself! You deserve it, and everyone you know will benefit from a healthier, happier you.

Sleep

Your voice can't survive or thrive without proper rest.

If you're tossing and turning or not even making it to bed most nights, there's probably something internal going on. In January of 2014, the Center for Disease Control (CDC) published a statement claiming sleep deprivation to be a public health epidemic with 50 to 70 million Americans experiencing some kind of sleep disorder.[1] A separate study by the Barna Group indicates that 58% of women and 70% of moms are tired, with accompanying emotional tolls including stress, a sense of being overwhelmed, and overall dissatisfaction with the work/home balance.[2]

I'm frequently asked about how I manage three children and my career. Most of the time, I have to be honest and say that I'm not really doing it very well.

When I had my children, I expected some sleepless nights. I was completely unprepared for night after night of interrupted sleep, restless sleep, no sleep . . . You get the idea. Most new parents can relate. And, to be honest, that's kind of part of parenthood in the early days. But it shouldn't be the trend when your kids are out of diapers and doing their thing. If you've got a five-year-old, why are you still waking up at all hours of the night?

It's beyond difficult to be a present parent and wife while striving to fulfill the professional or vocational call on your life. Oddly enough, CEOs and stay-at-home moms alike tend to wear sleep deprivation as a badge of honor. If we're sleeping less than anyone else, then we clearly must be working harder or giving more of ourselves, right?

We push and push our bodies to be the accomplished professional, PTA leader, attentive parent, loving wife . . . Somehow we've gotten this warped view that being a victim of our own ambition is virtuous. It shows that we are overcomers. We persevere!

So we keep playing the game. We overcommit. We worry about everything in the world even when it doesn't apply to us. We spend time on WebMD, self-diagnosing our imaginary problems into the wee hours, then hop on Facebook and see how we're stacking up to everyone we went to high school with. Before we know it, the sun is rising, and we're reaching for another overpriced Starbucks concoction or energy drink.

These habits cannot only be exhausting but seriously detrimental to our overall well-being and our relationships. More often than not, we don't realize how thin the ice is . . . until it begins to crack.

We get so out of the habit of a normal sleep pattern, it's almost as if we forget how to rest at all. That's when it's easy to resort to sleep aids—pills, tea, alcohol, sedatives—to counteract our energy medication. Our bodies become dependent on external, artificial regulators of sleep. While that may appear to work to our advantage professionally and socially, we're setting ourselves up for a major fall.

As ridiculous as it all sounds, it's happening all the time. We know it's crazy, but it somehow seems like less effort or more rewarding to keep up the crazy than to figure out a plan that's actually healthy and helps us achieve our true goals and desires—health, happiness, connectedness.

Sleep deprivation undoubtedly hinders work skills and mental clarity; for singers, sleep deprivation can end your career. A vocalist shouldn't expect much from his or her voice if adequate sleep and rest aren't happening. Your voice originates in the musculature surrounding your voice box. It is supported by breath. It depends on a lifted, supported diaphragm, and good posture. It is a very physical experience. It will be a compromised physical experience if the singer is exhausted. That's just science. Without adequate fuel and rest, a singer, an athlete, a mom, a wife, a person can't function optimally.

For those who are not singers or performers, the danger

signs of improper rest may be more subtle but can result in outcomes just as dire. Even if we know and understand what our God-given passions and ministries are, we can get so lost in the frenzy of doing them that we get tunnel vision. All we see is our goal, and we stubbornly push ahead, without even realizing we've left God and His wisdom far behind. It's only when we exhaust ourselves and collapse that we realize how far away we've wandered from everything and everyone. It seems as though we're completely alone and without a friend or support in the world. We see no compassion or warmth or kindness and, over time, harden our hearts in an attempt to survive. We accept fatigue, embrace our lone-warrior status, and carry on with our exhausting, solitary lives.

That's not what God wants for you or me or anyone. He wants you to have joy and hope and peace. He wants you to surrender the weight of your world to His hands. "Come to me, all you who are weary and burdened, and I will *give you rest*" (Matthew 11:28, emphasis mine).

Notice He doesn't guarantee here that He'll "take away" the things that burden us and make us weary—the diagnosis or the temptation or the high-pressure job. He says He will give us rest. Because it's when we are at rest, when we are stilled, when we are quiet that we can hear and receive and learn.

For many, it might be uncomfortable or even scary to be still and to rest. When you're still, you're surrendering control of your environment. If you define yourself by the things you do, doing nothing leads you to a conclusion that you are nothing. Some may feel unlovable if not for the services or products they can provide others. Their insecurity tells them that resting is not an option. It tells them they're lazy and worthless if they're not doing . . . something . . . all the time.

There are so many examples throughout the Bible of different ways God uses rest as a tool to get our attention or as a demonstration to teach us how to live. (The story of Mary and Martha [Luke 10:38–42] alone shows us how Jesus felt about living life with a go-go-go! attitude.) By taking a closer look at Scripture, we can begin to dispel the myths or misconceptions we've bought into throughout our lives. Perhaps if we can allow the following three truths to penetrate our thoughts, we can also let it transform our hearts.

1. Rest goes hand in hand with creation

God instituted a precedent of rest at the beginning of creation before the fall. Consider just how much more we need it now.

> Thus the heavens and the earth were completed in all their vast array.
>
> By the seventh day God had finished the work he had been doing; so on the seventh day he rested from all his work. Then God blessed the seventh day and made it holy, because on it he rested from all the work of creating that he had done. (Genesis 2:1–3)

Resting was part of the natural progression of behavior. God worked. He worked hard and well and was pleased with His creation, and then He rested. He established the natural order of human behavior in conjunction with the rest of creation, demonstrating priorities for us to follow.

That is critical for us to wrap our heads and our hearts around. It can be so difficult to believe that the rest is as important as the work. For so much of my life, I have defined myself by my career. I didn't know who I was without it. Therefore, resting was a terrifying prospect. But, everything God does is deliberate, and nothing in Scripture is a throwaway.

2. Rest leaves time for us to dream—and for God to speak

God emphasized rest not only for our health and well-being but because of its utility. He even frequently delivers messages during sleep.

In Genesis 28, we read about Jacob's dream of the stairway to heaven:

> He had a dream in which he saw a stairway resting on the earth, with its top reaching to heaven, and the angels of God were ascending and descending on it. There above it stood the LORD, and he said: "I am the LORD, the God of your father Abraham and the God of Isaac. I will give you and your descendants the land on which you are lying. Your descendants will be like the dust of the earth, and you will spread out to the west and to the east, to the north and to the south. All peoples on earth will be blessed through you and your offspring. I am with you and will watch over you wherever you go, and I will bring you back to this land. I will not leave you until I have done what I have promised you. (Genesis 28:12–15)

Joseph's entire life seems to be oriented around dreams. In adolescence, a dream set in motion the trajectory of the rest of his life (Genesis 37:5–9). After being sold by his brothers and then falsely accused and thrown into jail, his ability to interpret dreams eventually caused him to rise into Pharaoh's service (Genesis 40:8–23; 41:1–40), ultimately saving most of the world from starvation.

Skipping ahead to the New Testament, God chooses a dream to inform another Joseph, Mary's betrothed, about the goings-on of his pregnant bride-to-be (Matthew 1:20). Later, Joseph is warned in a dream about Herod's plan to kill Jesus and is able to get his wife and child to safety (Matthew 2:13).

I could go on and on about the use of dreams throughout Scripture, but you can see the point, that God uses them to deliver messages and get our attention. By communicating through dreams, He communicates when we are at rest. Consider the state of your sleep. Are you allowing God that window of communication? There have been periods in my life when I have been so busy and so on-edge that there wasn't a chance I would be sleeping long enough or well enough to attain the REM sleep state when dreams occur!

Now, maybe God doesn't speak to you in literal dreams, but I firmly believe that God often speaks to us today when we are in a place of rest. Dreams aside, I think we are to take a lesson from the obvious: each of these people are in a physical state of stillness and relaxation. When is our attention not being diverted in a thousand directions? When are we still? How can we expect or hope to receive anything in a state of agitation?

3. Rest clarifies and revives our purpose

If in the frenzy that is our lives we miss God's invitation to you or me today, that's all on us. He doesn't need us; He chooses us. It's up to us to lean in toward the sound of His voice.

There's a poignant example of this very thing in the book of John when Jesus encounters the Samaritan woman at the well.

Now Jesus learned that the Pharisees had heard that he was gaining and baptizing more disciples than

John—although in fact it was not Jesus who baptized, but his disciples. So he left Judea and went back once more to Galilee.

Now he had to go through Samaria. So he came to a town in Samaria called Sychar, near the plot of ground Jacob had given to his son Joseph. Jacob's well was there, and Jesus, tired as he was from the journey, sat down by the well. It was about noon.

When a Samaritan woman came to draw water, Jesus said to her, "Will you give me a drink?" (His disciples had gone into the town to buy food.)

The Samaritan woman said to him, "You are a Jew and I am a Samaritan woman. How can you ask me for a drink?" (For Jews do not associate with Samaritans.) (John 4:1–9)

From the outset, Jesus was leading by example. He was tired and knew His body needed to rest. While resting, He engaged beautifully in an act of grace, compassion, and love towards a woman who was undoubtedly weary and wary of this strange man, this Jew, who was defying social standards by even speaking to her, a Samaritan. This is not a footnote: this is a startling event. The fact that Jesus would talk to a woman has generated hundreds of commentaries and lessons. There's a story of racial segregation and unification in Jesus, the Jew, speaking to a Samaritan. There's a story of gender equality in here. Jesus, a man, addresses a woman. He speaks to her with dignity and respect.

As the conversation unfolds, Jesus explains the difference between Living Water and the water she was drawing from the well. He takes her out of her routine. He slows her down. He causes her to rest as well.

Jesus answered, "Everyone who drinks this water will be thirsty again, but whoever drinks the water I give them will never thirst. Indeed, the water I give them will become in them a spring of water welling up to eternal life."

The woman said to him, "Sir, give me this water so that I won't get thirsty and have to keep coming here to draw water." (John 4:13–15)

Here, Jesus throws a curveball. He asks about her husband, making bold statements about her previous relationships while asserting that even she—a Samaritan, an adulteress—is worthy to worship God.

He told her, "Go, call your husband and come back."

"I have no husband," she replied.

Jesus said to her, "You are right when you say you have no husband. The fact is, you have had five husbands, and the man you now have is not your husband. What you have just said is quite true."

"Sir," the woman said, "I can see that you are a prophet. Our ancestors worshiped on this mountain, but you Jews claim that the place where we must worship is in Jerusalem."

"Woman," Jesus replied, "believe me, a time is coming when you will worship the Father neither on this mountain nor in Jerusalem. You Samaritans worship what you do not know; we worship what we do know, for salvation is from the Jews. Yet a time is coming and has now come when the true worshipers will worship the Father in the Spirit and in truth, for they are the kind of worshipers the Father seeks. God is spirit, and

his worshipers must worship in the Spirit and in truth."
(John 4:16–24)

I don't think Jesus was trying to make her feel bad or shameful by bringing up her past. Rather, I think He did so to free her from it.

Have you ever done something so shameful you couldn't tell a soul? Have you carried with you a secret that haunts your heart and mind? If so, you know how exhausting it is to live that way. By naming her transgressions and demonstrating kindness and love towards her despite them, He's liberating her spirit. After so many years of carrying this burden of shame, He is lifting it from her shoulders.

The effect is profound. With a revived spirit and a new freedom, the woman rushed back into the town, extolling the wonders she had just witnessed to the people who, only hours before, had been a judge and jury she took great pains to avoid. Many theologians have called her the first evangelist.

Isn't that incredible! Here was a woman who thought she didn't matter anymore. Who had stopped using her voice. But Jesus had other plans for her, and that voice that was once silent led many to life and light.

> Many of the Samaritans from that town believed in him because of the woman's testimony, "He told me everything I ever did." So when the Samaritans came to him, they urged him to stay with them, and he stayed two days. And because of his words many more became believers.
>
> They said to the woman, "We no longer believe just because of what you said; now we have heard for ourselves, and we know that this man really is the Savior of the world." (John 4:39–42)

The lesson here is clear. First, it's okay to rest. Jesus models that by stopping at the well in the first place. Sure, he had places to go, things to do—but He opted to honor His body and give it the rest it needed.

Second, we can never truly engage in restorative rest with a shadow of guilt, regret, or secret sin lurking. It's when those things are brought to the light that we find rest. When our souls find peace, our voice can rise. This woman had hidden her voice from others for years. Yet when she was freed from the chains she had been dragging for so long, she used her voice to bring about change, freedom, and salvation.

> Come to me, all *you* who are weary and burdened,
> and I will *give you rest*. (Matthew 11:28, emphasis mine)

If you are afflicted with sleeplessness, it's time to reevaluate your perspective and practice of rest. Let's go back to Daniel here. Ten days. If you have kids, you put them on some type of sleep schedule when they were born. Not to delve into the effectiveness of said schedule on your children, but let's reconfigure the scenario a bit . . . time to put yourself on a schedule.

For the next ten days, map out your bedtime and wake-up time, and then adjust the rest of your life and schedule around that instead of sacrificing your sleep to accommodate your schedule. This might mean that something has to go. You might have to back out of a class or a committee or some type of commitment.

IT'S OKAY TO SAY NO.

One more time for impact.

IT'S OKAY TO SAY NO.

This is your ten-day experiment, remember? But I'm

guessing and hoping that you're going to start feeling the effects of being rested, and you will like them. The bottom line is that your body cannot run on empty. It must be nourished, hydrated, and rested. Artificial energy may carry you through a day or two, but it's nothing that can be sustained without incurring some significant damage. You simply have to decide to value yourself enough to make good decisions.

You would never feed your kids junk or dehydrate them or deny them of sleep.

Why do you do it to yourself?

You're God's child. That makes you valuable and absolutely deserving of good care.

EXERCISE AND ACTIVITY

*T*o sing well, regular vocal work and exercise are absolutely imperative. The muscles that produce vocal sound work the same way as the muscles that help you run. Work and challenge them regularly, and they stay strong. Neglect the workout, and they atrophy and can't do what you want them to. I can't just sing when it's time to do a show or go into the studio. I have to sing every day to maintain the quality and strength of my voice.

We all know that an object in motion tends to stay in motion. An object at rest tends to stay at rest. This is known as inertia. Physics 101.

Guess what . . . you're an object! Your body works the same way.

But . . . let me guess . . . you have no time.

I know. No one does! It may not be realistic to hit the gym for an hour every day, so get creative. There are so many ways to incorporate physical activity into your daily life.

Take the stairs.

Park in the last spot in the parking lot.

Jog in place while you fold laundry.

Or carve out an hour to hit the gym or the treadmill or watch any of countless workout videos you can find on YouTube.

Becoming an active person isn't difficult . . . once you begin.

It's the inertia concept.

Do you remember when recess or PE was your favorite part of the day? Why not bring recess back? This is your time to put on comfy clothes and shoes and let out your stress, frustration, and excitement . . . you'd be surprised what can fuel you in a kickboxing session once you open the floodgate.

Who knows . . . you might start having fun!

That should be a goal.

Life's too short to do workouts you hate or to stay on the couch because you're convinced you loathe working out.

Everyone is so different, it's hard to prescribe an ideal method for working exercise into your life beyond this—treat it like you would any other appointment. Write it into your calendar. Give yourself adequate time to change, shower afterwards, and whatever else you need to make it work. Above all, stop thinking that it's a selfish thing to do.

Women start to lose bone mass as early as their thirties. And that's in healthy women! For those who have struggled with any type of illness or condition, that can begin far younger. Lifting weights has been proven to help maintain and even build bone mass.[3] Osteoporosis isn't something you want or have time to mess around with. If your body is fragile and brittle, its physically capabilities are limited, which will have a snowball effect on everything else in your life.

Stop thinking of exercise as something you'll get to one day. It is just as imperative to good health as hydration. Give yourself time to find something you enjoy. Don't give up on yourself—find an activity you're good at or like to do. Your body and vitality is worth it.

> Do you not know that your bodies are temples of the Holy Spirit, who is in you, whom you have received from God? You are not your own; you were bought at a price. Therefore honor God with your bodies. (1 Corinthians 6:19–20)

What more needs to be said?

Get up, get moving, and stay in the game. We need you out here.

JUST SAY NO

*D*o you remember the DARE program or whatever "Just Say No" program your school championed growing up? All the examples portrayed the drug dealers as scary, scruffy guys in black trench coats and the drug-free people as beautiful and carefree. It didn't take long after sixth grade to realize that those portrayals weren't exactly accurate.

Generally, those substances which promise relief of some kind look pretty good to most people. Any beer or wine commercial will tell you that. The same could be said for cigarettes or pain pills, food, even shopping. These habits usually do offer some type of temporary respite. They wouldn't be addictive if they didn't. And in a world full of stress and demands and pain, we're all looking for relief.

I get the appeal! Thankfully, though, because of my faith, my profession, and my drive to succeed as a Christian singer, I've been motivated and supported to avoid a lot of those things. Professional singer and vocal coach Andrea Leap gives a general summation of why singers really should stay clean if they want to preserve their careers.

> "Anything that you put into your body is going to go right past your vocal cords. If you're a smoker, it's going to be harder to sing well; if you're drinking every night, it's going to be harder," she says. "I know some people who won't drink soda for that reason. I'm sure with Whitney Houston the larger issue was her overall health. That voice was an unbelievable instrument; it was going to take a lot to really undo it."[4]

Unfortunately, life gives us a lot. Whitney Houston had one of the greatest voices in history. She also had a tragic life. Her pain at home, in relationships, in places most of us will never know about, was stronger than her will to preserve her gift. She was so convinced she had to medicate to survive, she medicated past the point of feeling anything. When you're numb, nothing matters anymore. You drift away before anyone else even notices you're leaving.

Is anything really so terrible that your life isn't worth fighting for anymore? Is there really something that terrifies you to the point of choosing to feel nothing? If your answer is yes, you are not alone, and I am not in any position to judge or condemn you at all. In fact, if you're brave enough to say yes to that question, I commend you. There are so many people satisfied with staying in denial. Life is easier there.

But if you feel that it really is just too difficult to get

through a day without a glass or four of wine or a handful or more of pills, please get help. Today. Now. Close this book, get on the phone, and call someone. You are too precious and life is WAY too short to gamble that you'll be fine. You're not invincible. Even if abusing a substance doesn't directly take your life, it will put you in danger. Whitney Houston's official cause of death was drowning. She was numb, passed out, and the water took her where the pills left off.

Furthermore, substance abuse endangers others. I have a friend whose father was coming to see her for lunch. He was out on a motorcycle ride with three of his colleagues . . . and a professional truck driver was high, swerved into their lane, killed two of them, and took another man's leg.

Substances kill. If you're dabbling or you know someone who is, it's time to wake up. Sooner or later, you or someone you know will suffer heavily because of a substance. You have to be willing to eradicate them from your life or to acknowledge their power over other people.

I don't say any of this to scare you or to dramatize life any more than it already is. These same principles apply beyond alcohol or drugs. Maybe you engage in harmful relationships with men. Perhaps you're addicted to your social media stats. You might seek release in expensive purchases, excessive exercising, or serial friendships. Whatever it is that is a numbing agent in your life, it can easily overwhelm your heart, mind, and body.

As vigilantly as we protect our own children, don't you know God does the same for you? He knows every single thought in your head. He knows every single crack in your heart. He knows every single pill you may take or drink you may try to hide or problem in your friend you'd rather overlook. He is crying out to His children to live life with a clear head. It has nothing to do with a list of rules or being better or more moral than anyone else. It has *everything* to do with preserving your health and your life.

Truth is, if you're used to burying or numbing your sorrows with substances—or distracting yourself from your feelings with something as seemingly benign as a credit card or a pint of ice cream—it's going to hurt when you choose to stop. Your problems will still be there. And you need to be ready for that. But trust yourself enough to deal with your life. You're strong. You're brilliant and beautiful and you are never given more than you can handle (1 Corinthians 10:13). That's a promise to hang your heart on.

You need support in this. Don't expect to successfully walk away from a problem like this on your own. Whether your addiction revolves around pills or alcohol or food or shopping or gambling or sex . . . you will need help to remove it from your life.

There is no shame in reaching out.

FROM THE INSIDE OUT

So, now that you're primed and ready to be healthy, active, confident and strong, you've got to go out into a world that also wants you to look like Barbie.

Ugh.

Our culture has such a warped and unhealthy expectation of physical appearance. For years, I allowed an eating disorder to tell me how I was supposed to look. I let food and exercise and appearance torture me, until I finally realized one day that my eating disorder didn't want anything good for me. It sought to punish me for not being what I thought I should be. And I let it.

I personify my eating disorder here because the power that I handed over to it robbed so much of myself. I allowed it to become a dictator in my life. One that I could never please or satiate. It was a relentless voice that perpetuated inadequacy and destruction.

That's the last thing God wants for us.

The great thing about reclaiming your health is that your body will be affected by it.

Sooner or later, a healthier diet, good rest, and exercise will change your size, your complexion, your hair . . . all of it will improve. When your physical health improves, your mental well-being will likewise see benefits. When you're giving your brain what it needs, it can much more clearly realize that magazine covers and fashion runways are unrealistic. It should make no sense to deprive yourself or try to manipulate your nutrition or body to achieve something that never existed in the first place.

> "And why do you worry about clothes? See how the flowers of the field grow. They do not labor or spin. Yet I tell you that not even Solomon in all his splendor was dressed like one of these. If that is how God clothes the grass of the field, which is here today and tomorrow is thrown into the fire, will he not much more clothe you— you of little faith?" (Matthew 6:28–30)

God knows that your appearance matters. He knitted you together, and He makes no mistakes. You're a masterpiece. Whatever size, shape, color you are . . . you're perfect. You were made by Him, for Him. And I don't think God's in the business of creating damaged goods.

I know that it's easy to know that in your head, and then

to look in the mirror or at the scale and let that resolve come crashing down. But as much as you have to condition your voice or your body to perform, you have to condition your mind to do the same. Keep telling yourself that you are beautiful and perfect just the way you are until it starts to become second nature. Put encouraging quotes or verses on the mirror to greet you in the morning. Make strategic choices about the magazines on your table and the media you consume. Affirm your beauty and your "enough-ness" until you believe it.

Negative self-talk is sneaky and destructive—and not only to the individual engaging in it. Over the years, I've put my husband in the unnecessarily awkward position of having to defend his wife—to his wife! We've had way too many conversations in which he's trying to convince me that I'm not ugly or heavy or inadequate. At the end of each one, he's saying the thing I want to hear—"You are beautiful and strong and talented"—but he's exhausted. The sweet words aren't delivered sweetly but in exasperation and frustration. In the course of my attack on myself, I've communicated to him that the love and affirmation he's tried to give to and show me aren't enough. Despite his efforts, I still feel terrible about myself, which leaves now not just one person (me) feeling inadequate, but two.

Now, what do you think our kids are seeing, hearing, and trying to process? If there's one parenting-ism that I've discovered is true 100 percent of the time, it's that kids miss nothing. My daughters know if Mommy feels fat or ugly or down. What they may not know, especially when they're young, is that Mommy sometimes says things that just aren't true. In their eyes, Mommy is up there with Elsa and Anna and any other princess they revere. If Mommy says she's fat, from their perspective, there's an element of truth to that. And if Mommy's fat, what does that mean about their bodies, now or in the future?

The things that we say are a reflection of the way we think and feel. All three elements—our speech, our thoughts, and our feelings—shape and impact every relationship we have. Even when we direct those messages internally, the impact is never self-contained. It's kind of like dropping a rock in a lake. You may be the only person who gets splashed, but the ripples can be felt even hundreds of feet away.

If you engage in negative self-talk or feel badly about yourself, you are not a villain. Feeling bad about yourself doesn't make you a bad person. As someone who's struggled with low self-esteem and lack of self-worth, the last thing I would ever want to do is make you feel worse about yourself. The truth remains, however, that those patterns, by design, don't work.

In Philippians 4:8, Paul writes, "Finally, brothers and sisters, whatever is true, whatever is noble, whatever is right, whatever is pure, whatever is lovely, whatever is admirable—if anything is excellent or praiseworthy—think about such things."

As beautiful a sentiment as that is, he didn't include it just to sound eloquent. If you keep reading, Paul expresses his gratitude to the Philippians for sympathizing with and supporting him, clarifying the intent of his letter in verse 17. "Not that I desire your gifts; what I desire is that more be credited to your account."

He's looking out for them. He wants the best for them. And he knows that the best is God's best, hence his suggestion in verse 8. His desire is for them to live and experience the best life possible. He knows that their thoughts and feelings and the direction of their mental focus is key to such a life. We were designed to work best when we're thinking and focusing on good things.

The reverse is also true. We can't function optimally when our minds are weighed down by self-deprecating thoughts or any type of defeating mindset.

As a woman who has struggled with body issues and eating disorders, I've learned that I must choose every day to embrace myself the way God made me. I actually struggle almost daily with those feelings of insecurity. Over the years, though, I've noticed a pattern. When I'm focusing more on myself, I struggle more. When I focus on God, I struggle less. I have to hide His word in my heart so that when the negative voices arise I have an arsenal of truth to extinguish them.

It's a tactic I've relied on over the years and one I hope to impress upon my daughters. I now try to limit talking about how I look in front of them. I've also made a very conscious effort to take care of myself physically.

Instead of going on a diet, though, I overhauled my entire lifestyle to include healthy amounts of exercise and good, clean, and nourishing food. I lost a lot of weight, this time in a healthy way, but my goal is not a size; it is to normalize healthy living in my home.

It's an act of worship to properly care for our bodies. I want my girls to realize the intrinsic benefits of good health and not approach food or exercise as merely a means to fit a cultural mold of the ideal. We have made exercise and physical activity part of our family life. We do it together. In the long run, we're not only strengthening our bodies; we're fortifying our bond as mother and daughter, husband and wife.

So what does all this mean for you? I'm not really the one to decide. It's likely an action plan you will need to develop with informed input from a doctor, coach, counselor, spouse, relative, or friend. I'm not an expert, but I at least hope the suggestions I've included in this chapter may prompt you towards a life that's free from self-condemnation, filled with pride in the beauty of God's creation (that would be you!), and focused on the joy of living.

CLOTHED IN STRENGTH AND HONOR

*W*hen it comes to our overall appearance, we'd be wise to remember that everything we do—the clothes we wear, our modesty, or lack thereof—matters. There are eyes on you at all times.

That said, you shouldn't be dressing to appease any one person or group of people. They are not the end-all, be-all. God is. Dress in a way that honors Him.

I don't mean in an interview or corporate office setting only. If you're an entertainer, you should wear stage clothes that don't distract from your message. Off-stage, you should do the same. If you're a stay-at-home mom, dress in a manner that's practical, but affirms that it's okay to take care of and spend some time on yourself.

Here are a few things I keep in mind when I'm choosing my clothes for the stage, the bus, home on the weekend, or anywhere else. Through these guidelines, I find it easier to express myself, respect myself, and be an example.

- Look at your Bible instead of the mirror. Start your day staring at Him . . . I'm confident your mind will begin to change when you put His face before your own.
- Stop giving numbers so much power. If you are preoccupied with the scale, ditch it. You can even ask your doctor for blind weigh-ins when you're there for check-ups. I know a woman who had struggled with

eating disorders for years. When she began to heal, she stopped looking at scales . . . even through two pregnancies. As long as you are in the general care of a physician, and as long as those numbers are doing more harm than good, look away. There's a lot of freedom there.

- Don't accept the entertainment industry's falsified version of "normal." You already know that photo-shopping is the norm when it comes to popular culture and the way women are portrayed. Use that knowledge to free yourself from those bizarre, unhealthy standards. It's not real—therefore we should give those kinds of images no power at all over our psyche and self-perception. We all talk about the edited images on magazine covers, yet we try to achieve it anyway. Those images have less to do with the model or actress they portray than the graphic designer who deleted imperfections and made that person whatever size they thought would sell the most magazines. Those covers are art projects. Accept it, even laugh at it, and move on.

- Find clothes and a style that's you and makes you feel beautiful. Style matters! It can be a source of pride and creativity. If you're going to dwell on your appearance, start thinking in terms of expressing who you are through your clothes. It's a lot healthier than just grabbing something black because it's slimming . . . or buying clothes that aren't really you because so-and-so on the cover of *InStyle* claimed it was the "in" item of the season.

- I love to throw together different outfits that show off my personality and flatter the figure God gave me.

When it comes to the stage, I want to be current but not trendy. In everyday life, I greatly value functionality and versatility, so I frequently opt for layers. If your closet is filled with a few basics of high quality, you can then mix and match, accessorize, and otherwise spice things up with ease.

- One size fits all is a myth! Your body is different from anyone else's. Wear clothes that highlight your favorite features and flatter your unique shape.

- Don't focus on the tag. Cut it out if you have to. Even within the same brand, clothing size varies. In other words, a pair of GAP jeans may be perfect for you in a size 8. However, their size-8 dress isn't quite right. Don't beat yourself up if you're not wearing the size you think you should be wearing. Clothing size is relative. In any scenario the best fit for you is what fits the best.

- Try to smile. Take it from Little Orphan Annie . . . You're never fully dressed without a smile. Even if you have to fake it till you feel it, try to smile and laugh. The physical act releases endorphins that may actually make you feel better and happier. Happiness is beautiful.

Your impact on others in life is only strengthened by your capacity to be healthy and present yourself in a way that honors God and yourself. Be proud of who you are. Fight for your health. Allow yourself to take care of yourself, and stop apologizing for doing so.

From the inside out, what you consume, do, or wear will impact your success, happiness, and overall well-being. Honor the temple that the Lord created you to be. Care for the body He placed you in and do so with gratitude.

Do you not know that your bodies are temples of the Holy Spirit, who is in you, whom you have received from God? You are not your own; you were bought at a price. Therefore honor God with your bodies. (1 Corinthians 6:19–20)

He shed His blood for you—not an alternate or idealized version of you. He created you to be His and to honor Him with every beat of your heart. It's up to you to take the initiative and honor His creation. Seek not a reflection that is thin enough, pretty enough, chic enough; seek His face. That's where matchless worth and beauty lie.

Chapter 6

ALIGNING YOUR ASSETS

───────── *so* ─────────

*A*re you a sing-in-the-shower person? Or do you sing in the car with all the windows rolled up, avoiding eye contact with the car stopped next to you at the red light, determined not to let an inquisitive glance deter your big solo? (I'm both!)

If you're more of a shower singer, you might notice that it is, in general, a lot easier to sing out loud and clear and annoy your family when you're standing than when you're sitting in a car. Because of our body's design, air flows more freely and singing is better supported when we are standing or sitting up nice and straight than when bent or stooped over.

Today, I'm vigilant about my posture when I sing. I have to engage every muscle correctly in order to maximize my sound without hurting my vocal cords. Unfortunately, I had to learn that the hard way. For years, I simply relied on raw talent when it came to singing. I have what some refer to as 'vocal chords of steel.' In other words, I have a voice that stays strong regardless of how I abuse it. I never had any formal vocal training and just relied on my natural ability and a "help me Jesus" here and there to get me through. I didn't pay attention to technique because I honestly didn't know it, and I eventually paid the price, developing nodes on my vocal cords (nasty little bumps that inhibit your capacity to sing). I've also lost my voice on nearly every single tour I've done throughout my career—until this most recent one.

Finally, after years of winging it, hoping that my voice would miraculously withstand anything, I realized I was threatening my future, so I needed to start doing things properly. So, after years on the road, several albums and five awards for Gospel music's Female Vocalist of the Year, I decided to get some vocal training. Better late than never, right?

Remarkably, I've learned so much already from my vocal coach. It's imperative to have someone speak wisdom into your life and craft. Like I said, this past year is the first tour of my career that I haven't lost my voice. I'm finally putting together the pieces of proper posture, alignment, and control.

When I'm singing, I have to be able to access and engage my diaphragm with ease. The diaphragm is a muscle that stretches across the stomach area and supports breathing. When correctly used, it supports a full, beautiful, warm tone. If I'm slouching or not focusing on engaging that muscle, the result is a vocal tone that's thin and much more difficult to control.

In real life, you are shortchanging yourself and your capacity to be productive, successful, healthy, and happy if your alignment is off. Your life's posture will enable you to either breathe deeply the richness of life or it will force you to sip shallow, frantic breaths just to make it through. You can probably guess which of the two is going to lead to a greater sense of empowerment and confidence.

Let's illustrate this with an experiment: Wherever you are right now, slouch down. Don't even attempt good posture here.

Now, take a deep breath and let it out slowly.

Do it again.

Now, take five short breaths one after the other. Repeat.

One more deep breath in and out.

Next, sit up straight. Look straight ahead, square your shoulders, and do the same breathing exercise.

Notice anything?

In either position, I'm sure the slow breathing seemed more fulfilling than the fast breaths. But isn't it amazing how much of a difference sitting up straight made? You're smart; you know why. Your lungs and diaphragm need room to expand and take in your breath. When you're slouching, they have far less room to expand.

One more experiment.

Resume the slouching position. Breathe as well as you can and sing a song. "Happy Birthday," "Jesus Loves Me," whatever . . .

Then sit up straight and do it again.

Pretty remarkable, right? (And now you can understand why your high school choir director incessantly told you to sit up straight. God bless high school choir directors.)

Even if you are doing your best to breathe well, if you aren't sitting up straight, your breath doesn't have an ally. Your lungs won't be able to expand, and your diaphragm won't be able to use the breath efficiently. The reverse is also true. If you're sitting up straight with great posture but are breathing incorrectly, you're not going to get great results. Your breath and your posture aren't working together. They are not aligned, ultimately compromising the control you have over your voice and possibly causing injury. It's like a car. If the alignment is off, the tires wear out more quickly, gas efficiency goes way down, and it's harder to steer.

Nothing I've said thus far is probably a surprise to you. It's pretty obvious that if you don't use something correctly, you're going to break it eventually. Many times, though, head knowledge doesn't translate to our hearts and hands. We probably know the right thing or the right way to do something, but, for whatever reason, come up with an alternative that we think is more fun, interesting, or just better overall.

For example, in honor of National Karaoke Week—yes there is such a thing—mentalfloss.com published an article listing the fifteen most requested karaoke songs. Michael Jackson's "Billie Jean" took the top spot, followed by songs from Weezer,[1] Natalie Imbruglia, Journey, Adele, Madonna . . . and the list went on. We love to sing big! And why wouldn't we? Every singer listed here is phenomenal. Who wouldn't want to sound like them?

That list makes me laugh, thinking about my own turns at the karaoke table throughout the years. It never mattered if the song was in my range or suited for my voice. If it were a song I loved, I'd go for it and then be hoarse for the rest of the week. At the time, I could afford to ignore my tessitura and sing all over the place, far beyond my thrive zone. Today, I don't have that option. I can't afford to have a week with my voice not at its peak—the stakes are too high. I make my living singing on a stage or in a studio; if my voice is shot, I'm out of commission. I have to take care of it, and I have to use it correctly.

The same principle applies to relationships, professional decisions, and our overall lifestyle. You can cut corners here and there without significant ramifications—especially when you're young. As you go through life, though, and start building a family and networks of people who depend on you, the stakes are higher. You can't be careless with people and expect relationships to bounce back every time. Eventually, you may cause damage that can't be undone.

So how do you prevent it? Get the mechanics down. Learn how to live your life in alignment with God and His word, and practice it every day.

You can take a car to a shop and pay someone to whip that alignment back into shape.

For your life, you're going to have to work harder than that and be intentional.

One of my favorite people in history and Scripture is David. Shepherd David. Musician David. Warrior David. King David. Adulterer David. Murderer David. Contrite David. Man-after-God's-own-heart David.

We see David revealed in so many dimensions throughout the Bible. His character development is among the most complete of anyone in Scripture. We see him win and lose. We see him make both excellent and horrific decisions, and we see the fallout and blessing of it all.

When we see him for the very first time, he personifies proper alignment. Young David had it together on a level so beyond most people that he was able to defeat impossible foes.

Even later in life, when David is at his worst—adultery, murder, subterfuge—because he was still fundamentally aligned with God, he was able to find his way back through contrition, confession, and redemption.

But it started with a young man, some stones, a sling, and a giant . . .

STANDING TALL

*D*avid and Goliath is the ultimate underdog story. Quick recap . . . The Israelites haven't been doing so well. The king that they had begged for, Saul, had fallen out of God's favor for not obeying specific orders. So a new king had been anointed who would assume the throne following Saul's death.

David is the new king-elect. As a young shepherd and

musician, he doesn't command an imposing presence. More likely than not, he was rather slight of stature, particularly compared to the great warriors of the Philistines. But David shows us all that it's not your stature that determines how tall you can stand. And he did so in the most unlikely of scenarios.

Saul had summoned David to play his harp. Saul had sleep issues, but David's music soothed him. One reason Saul was restless: a giant Philistine army camped way too close for comfort, preparing to pounce on the weakened Israeli nation. And they had a formidable weapon.

> A champion named Goliath, who was from Gath, came out of the Philistine camp. His height was six cubits and a span. He had a bronze helmet on his head and wore a coat of scale armor of bronze weighing five thousand shekels; on his legs he wore bronze greaves, and a bronze javelin was slung on his back. His spear shaft was like a weaver's rod, and its iron point weighed six hundred shekels. His shield bearer went ahead of him. (1 Samuel 17:4–7)

And then this giant shouted out a challenge. He told Israel to send out their best man to fight him, one-on-one. If Goliath killed the Israelite, the Israelite army would become slaves for the Philistines. But if the Israelite killed Goliath, the Philistines would be their servants.

If, like me, you're not up on your cubit conversion skills, six cubits and a span is equivalent to about 9 feet, 9 inches. Not surprisingly, there wasn't a line of Israelis lining up to take Goliath on. Although, the prize for anyone who did bring him down was pretty sweet—money, the king's daughter, and no more taxes for that warrior's family.

David was the youngest of his father's sons, and they didn't seem to have much affinity for him. I would presume that watching their younger brother being anointed to rule over them had something to do with that. Regardless, his brothers were soldiers, and David's father, Jesse, asked David to take some food down to them at the battle site and bring back an update.

David did as his father requested, and while there, Goliath showed up and threw his daily challenge out. David heard it and got an idea. At this point, something odd happened in the story that I had never paid much attention to when I was younger.

> David asked the men standing near him, "What will be done for the man who kills this Philistine and removes this disgrace from Israel? Who is this uncircumcised Philistine that he should defy the armies of the living God?"
>
> They repeated to him what they had been saying and told him, "This is what will be done for the man who kills him."
>
> When Eliab, David's oldest brother, heard him speaking with the men, he burned with anger at him and asked, "Why have you come down here? And with whom did you leave those few sheep in the wilderness? I know how conceited you are and how wicked your heart is; you came down only to watch the battle." (1 Samuel 17:26–28)

I hadn't noticed his brother's comment before. Seems a bit harsh to me! It probably wasn't the first time David heard something like that from his brothers. Nonetheless, he brushed it off and volunteered to battle this gigantic person, only to be met with Saul's comment: "You are not able to go out against this Philistine and fight him; you are only a young man, and he has been a warrior from his youth" (1 Samuel 17:33).

All excellent points! But David is not deterred.

> But David said to Saul, "Your servant has been keeping his father's sheep. When a lion or a bear came and carried off a sheep from the flock, I went after it, struck it and rescued the sheep from its mouth. When it turned on me, I seized it by its hair, struck it and killed it. Your servant has killed both the lion and the bear; this uncircumcised Philistine will be like one of them, because he has defied the armies of the living God. The LORD who rescued me from the paw of the lion and the paw of the bear will rescue me from the hand of this Philistine."
>
> Saul said to David, "Go, and the LORD be with you."
> (1 Samuel 17:34–37)

There is so much to unpack here, and the battle hasn't even begun!

The most obvious thing going on is the absurdity of David's idea. He's a small shepherd who plays the harp.

Goliath is 9'9".

Again . . . 9'9".

Shaquille O'Neal is 7'1". Lebron James is 6'8". Gheorghe Mureşan and Manute Bol are on record as the tallest players in NBA history. They were both 7'7".

Goliath is nine feet, nine inches tall!

That's ridiculous!

Surely people questioned David's sanity in even thinking of taking on this giant.

But David was confident. He assumed a posture of faith

in his God and knew He could complete the task. He also rose above the naysayers. Standing straight, looking up, David relied on the Spirit, which had come upon him in the previous chapter when Samuel found and anointed David, per God's instructions: "So Samuel took the horn of oil and anointed him in the presence of his brothers, and from that day on the Spirit of the LORD came powerfully upon David" (1 Samuel 16:13).

That's important to know. He didn't just happen to hear from God on battle day. He'd been soaking up the Spirit of the Lord for some time.

Frequently, when we get in a tight spot, we ask God to swoop in and save the day. When things go south, we get mad and blame Him when we fall. Cue the adult temper tantrum. Our fists may clench; our jaw may tighten up. We often avert our eyes above or to the side of whoever is the target of our anger. Our entire bodies go rigid.

Anger isn't the only emotion that can wreak havoc on our physiological state. When we are nervous, scared, or insecure, our physical response nearly mirrors that of anger. Our heart rate increases, our breathing becomes more frantic, and our bodies go tense.

Good luck trying to sing in that position. You will not be able to get the air you need if your body is taut. What is possible is to train your body to rise above that emotional stance. If you are in the discipline of aligning your body in the appropriate position, muscle memory eventually kicks in, and before long, you can make your body do what you want it to do despite how you're feeling.

Should a situation arise in which God isn't answering or giving you what you think He should, you'll tense up. You may start fortifying those walls around your heart so that nothing painful or frustrating can get in. You'll assume a posture the opposite of that of humility, praise, faith, and trust. You'll distance yourself from God and make it virtually impossible to breathe in His fragrance and love.

Fortunately, you don't have to stay that way. Just like in singing, you can be in the practice of staying malleable, available, and trusting. When times are good, when your faith feels fresh and exciting, get in the habit of prayer, church, fellowship, and support. Discipline yourself to make these things a part of your life as soon as you are able. It becomes immensely difficult to incorporate that approach to life when things are already bad. Daily, assume a posture of humility, and keep doing so even when you don't want to. Keep praying even if you don't know what to say.

Keep going to a church or a Bible study or any kind of place of ministry where you'll at least hear the truth of God.

Eventually your discipline will lead you through the fog by doing what only a posture of humility and faith do—keep you close enough to God to breathe Him in.

Just as proper singing posture enables you to achieve the breath you need, proper spiritual posture allows you to breathe deeply of His essence.

It doesn't happen overnight. And if you're already past the honeymoon phase with God, that's okay. It's never too late.

David is such a beautiful example of someone who knew who he wanted to be—a protector, a warrior, a king. His upright posture helped him to stand apart from the very first time he appears in Scripture.

> He was glowing with health and had a fine appearance and handsome features.
> Then the LORD said, "Rise and anoint him; this is the one."

So Samuel took the horn of oil and anointed him in the presence of his brothers, and from that day on the Spirit of the LORD came powerfully upon David. (1 Samuel 16:12–13)

Believing that victory was possible through God was second nature for him. When the time came, David was ready and able to make that leap of faith. He wasn't pulled down by his brother's snarky comments nor Saul's expression of doubt.

What may have seemed like arrogance or idiocy was a natural progression of solid faith and discipline and certainty of calling. Goliath was tall, but David's posture of faith and humility placed him in a position to call upon God Almighty for victory.

BREATHING DEEP

*B*reathing is our first and last action in this world. It was the first action of mankind! Breath, inextricably connected to life, happens initially as an unconscious, natural process.

Vocal instructor Karyn O'Connor says: "We are born knowing how to breathe properly, and no one has to teach us how to do it when we come out of the womb. The tummies of sleeping babies rise and fall effortlessly, without any tension or movement in their chests and shoulders. The parts of their bodies that support their breathing work in effortless coordination and synchronicity. Even the breathing of adults is correct when they are relaxed or asleep and not actively trying to control it. The body naturally knows what to do and how to do it." The body knows this because this is how we were created. "Then the LORD God formed a man from the dust of the ground and *breathed* into his nostrils the breath of life, and the man became a living being" (Genesis 2:7, emphasis mine).

Unfortunately, our body forgets how to keep grounded to that life-giving breath, or we forget to pay attention to it. Somewhere between childhood and adolescence, we begin to override our autonomic function. We learn to deny or ignore our natural instincts, and instead of being relaxed so we can breathe freely, we constrict. We hold tension in our shoulders and our chests and get by on shallow gulps of air, even though it compromises how we feel, sound, and live.

For singers, proper breathing technique is fundamental. The best posture in the world can't compensate for poor breath support. Your range will suffer, your delivery will suffer, and you could potentially do a lot of damage to your vocal chords. Without that support, there will be notes that you can only reach by straining. That's not sustainable technique.

The same is true in your life. If you are living at a frenetic, breakneck speed, when do you ever catch your breath? Do you?

My guess is that you don't, nor do you ever even think about it. You, me, all of us have been conditioned to run on empty, simply surviving. We don't learn to listen to our bodies or our hearts to even learn the signs that we need to rest or breathe or be free of something.

Just like posture, proper breathing is a skill that must be learned and honed with practice. Singers and athletes both have to practice proper breathing so that in the moment of competition or performance, their nerves won't get the best of them and their breath will give them the fuel they need.

Let's revisit David. Here's this very young man who usually has a harp or follows his sheep. Now, he's about to battle

Goliath. Can you imagine how fast his heart must have been pounding? Do you think he was scared?

He certainly doesn't show it.

There was no going back. David had announced to the army, the Philistines, and the king that he was going to take on the mammoth of a man everyone else was too scared to confront.

Do you think there was a moment that David second-guessed his decision? I know I would, but for some reason, I doubt he did. The idea was so absurd to begin with—this young shepherd taking on the greatest warrior on the opposing team. He wouldn't have showed up had he not been completely committed from the start.

So there he is. No military training. No practice time. But standing with his eyes on the God he knows will bring victory, David assumed a posture of readiness. Ready to do what seemed impossible. Ready to believe in the gifts God had bestowed upon him and trust that God's word was true. Since Samuel had anointed him, David had disciplined himself to stand tall and breathe deep the fragrance of God.

When he announced that he would be the giant slayer, it didn't matter what anyone else said or did to deter him. He was ready . . . ready to accomplish this task with his God on God's terms.

Then Saul dressed David in his own tunic. He put a coat of armor on him and a bronze helmet on his head. David fastened on his sword over the tunic and tried walking around, because he was not used to them.

"I cannot go in these," he said to Saul, "because I am not used to them." So he took them off. Then he took his staff in his hand, chose five smooth stones from the stream, put them in the pouch of his shepherd's bag and, with his sling in his hand, approached the Philistine. (1 Samuel 17:38–40)

That took some major bravado to take off the king's tunic and armor in front of both armies. Scripture doesn't mention that Saul felt slighted in any way, but the subtext tells me that it could have been a very awkward situation. Regardless, David knew that his success would come from God and from the experiences and lessons God had taught him throughout his life. He didn't rely on the king's armor when he had the Creator's Spirit within him. In this moment of potential anxiety and fear, David's spiritual muscle memory kicked in, and he breathed in deeply the life-giving oxygen that is faith.

David knew the king's armor and tactics were useless to him. He didn't waiver. He took a deep breath, gathered his sling and stones, and began making his way towards the biggest battle he had yet faced, confident that the battle had already been won.

GAINING CONTROL

*W*hen is the last time you attended a concert and thought, "Wow. Look at that posture," or "That is some serious breathing."

Probably never, right?

Of course not. You're not going to watch someone stand up straight or breathe properly. You're going to have an experience. Be it a worship session or a rock concert or a theatrical performance, you are there for the full experience.

As a vocalist, your goal is for your voice to look and sound effortless. When you achieve this, you can let your music do what only music can do . . . tell a story to the whole world, one person at a time. If and when that happens, you've created something far beyond entertainment; you've begun a relationship. You've eliminated the "me" and "them" paradigm. Your stage is now their stage. Your song is now their song, a song that has become part of the soundtrack of their lives. Because you've invoked an emotional response, you've now become more than a musician. You've become their companion, that person in their lives they can turn to for comfort, empathy, or encouragement. You've given them the gift of togetherness, reassuring them that whatever they are going through, they're not doing it alone.

But there is a giant "if" to all of this. If your fundamental skills are shaky, you cannot achieve optimal vocal control, which is founded on mechanics. Be it your physical stance or your breathing, if one is off, your delivery will suffer, reducing the impact of the experience. You risk losing connection with people and an opportunity for your music to become part of their lives.

That's not to say that only perfection will resonate with an audience. However, more often than not, the audience will focus on whatever commands *your* focus. If your attention is consumed by your pitch or lyrics or the tuning on your guitar because you are not adequately prepared, the audience may soon be thinking about the same things. If you have to pay attention to those basics, you won't be fully invested in the performance, impeding others from doing so also.

The same principles apply to life. If your posture is off—if your pride or self-interest prohibit a position of humility and faith—you won't be able to breathe in the love and truth of Christ. It's easy to get distracted when you give priority to protecting your reputation or projecting a certain image. Perhaps you end up fixating on your family's image, your home decor, your appearance, or your salary. As I said before, when I fixate on myself, things go south. When I focus on Him, everything in my life is better. Without faith and without Christ, you are playing Russian roulette. You may be on top of things one day and feel completely in control, and the next you could spiral.

We see this juxtaposition in Goliath. Goliath was like an arrogant celebrity athlete. He was at the top; he'd always been at the top and how dare this little person challenge him. He immediately dismissed David as a valid threat, which weakened his defenses.

David, on the other hand, knew that if he was even going to survive this matchup, much less win it, he was going to need some help. The dialogue between the two certainly says it all.

[Goliath] looked David over and saw that he was little more than a boy, glowing with health and handsome, and he despised him. He said to David, "Am I a dog, that you come at me with sticks?" And the Philistine cursed David by his gods. "Come here," he said, "and I'll give your flesh to the birds and the wild animals!"

David said to the Philistine, "You come against me with sword and spear and javelin, but I come against you in the name of the LORD Almighty, the God of the armies of Israel, whom you have defied. This day the LORD will deliver you into my hands, and I'll strike you down and cut off your head. This very day I will give the carcasses of the Philistine army to the birds and the wild animals, and the whole world will know that there is a God in Israel. All those gathered here will know that it is not

by sword or spear that the LORD saves; for the battle is
the LORD's, and he will give all of you into our hands."
(1 Samuel 17:42–47)

David talked a great game, and I can only guess that his
delivery matched. I imagine his posture must have been erect,
his voice well-supported and convincing. He was unlike anyone who had challenged Goliath before, and Goliath's go-to
responses and retaliations just didn't seem to generate the
usual fear. David asserted his confidence, assuming control.

What happens next convinces me that David's presentation must have been at least enough to throw something off
inside Goliath.

As the Philistine moved closer to attack him, David
ran quickly toward the battle line to meet him. Reaching
into his bag and taking out a stone, he slung it and struck
the Philistine on the forehead. The stone sank into his
forehead, and he fell face down on the ground.

So David triumphed over the Philistine with a sling
and a stone; without a sword in his hand he struck down
the Philistine and killed him. (1 Samuel 17:48–50)

A stone.

A stone brought down this warrior who had been fighting
since childhood. I somehow doubt that this was the first time
he'd had something lobbed at his head. I bet he had ducked out
of the way of other flying objects in his lifetime.

But something was different this time. An intangible force
that changed the game permanently . . .

David had control of the situation from the beginning,
and he never faltered. Like a vocalist who commands a stage,

his posture was right on, his breathing steady, deep, and supported. He optimized his assets and allowed God to work through him, which led to an outcome far greater than one he could have engineered on his own. He won the day because he paid attention to the small things that make the difference between victory and defeat.

As you continue to find and refine your voice, bear in mind the necessity of proper alignment. Stand up straight and keep your eyes focused on the One who will help you remain firm, solid, and grounded regardless of any other circumstance in your life. A heart aligned with God's will always beats stronger than one going it alone. If we merely put the work in and discipline ourselves to be in line with His thoughts and will, close enough to breathe in His essence, no giant can defeat us.

Now that's something worth singing in the shower about.

Chapter 7

QUALITY CHECK: IT'S HOW YOU SAY IT

———— &0 ————

*W*hen I was growing up, I knew singing would always be a big part of my life. I loved listening to artists of any genre and recreating those sounds with my own voice. Over time, I realized that I didn't have to imitate anyone else or attempt to manufacture another artist's sound. The tone and texture of my voice were very different than most other women in the Christian music genre.

I had spent much of my life listening to and being influenced by soul music. I just love how every single note drips with emotion. Growing up in Seattle, the birthplace of grunge, my friends were all listening to Pearl Jam, while I was the blonde-hair, blue-eyed girl singing Aretha Franklin, Stevie Wonder, and the Winans into my hairbrush. As I continued to grow and develop my singing skills, I learned to incorporate a more soulful style into my own individual sound. As I began my journey in the contemporary Christian music genre, that made me unique but also difficult to classify in an industry that employs pretty cut-and-dried categories—pop, rock, gospel, and so on.

I think because I allow my voice to explore various nuances

and tones, I am able to sing different kinds of songs that appeal to diverse audiences. Over the years, I've discovered ways to maximize those qualities and embrace, enhance, and celebrate my unique sound. I've also learned ways to adjust my tone and texture for different environments. I'm going to deliver a song at the pregame Super Bowl show much differently than I would lead a worship song at a church. Neither style is less of who I am, nor is it a compromise. Rather, it's a product of life experience and vocal maturity.

As a performer, your goal is to make people experience something. You want them to fall in love to your songs or cry away a heartbreak to your voice. You want them to celebrate salvation and experience redemption through your music. That's what music is—a vessel of emotion. Understanding and effectively executing appropriate tone and texture enables you to connect. Without it, you're just singing notes. Music is more substantial than mere execution.

In the era of emojis, texting, memes, twitter, Instagram, and the like, we are gradually falling out of practice when it comes to expressing genuine emotion. You can't interject real happiness or sadness in a text message. Nor can you exude encouragement through a little yellow smiley face alone. As the quality of our communication deteriorates and the context becomes increasingly impersonal, relationship quality follows suit.

A study conducted at UCLA found that sixth-graders who went five days without looking at a phone, television, or other screen did much better at reading human emotions than kids from the same school in the same grade who continued to use their devices at will.[1] At times, it feels like the majority of culture is regressing in the area of emotional intelligence.

When a singer stands on stage and sings notes disconnected

from a meaning or melody, the audience is quickly going to be bored. The same happens when we simply fill silence or pretend to listen to others. We grow apathetic to people around us or pull back and isolate. It's a sad way to go through life and ultimately a destructive pattern.

We weren't made to live in isolation. God gave us a deep pool of emotions, meant to be shared with others. What a shame to let them go to waste.

ONCE MORE, WITH FEELING

*L*et's return to one of the masters of quality control and emotional intelligence that we see in the Bible: Joseph. Of course, he didn't start out this way. Early on, he learned the adverse effects that arise from thoughtless communication.

Now Israel loved Joseph more than any of his other sons, because he had been born to him in his old age; and he made an ornate robe for him. When his brothers saw that their father loved him more than any of them, they hated him and could not speak a kind word to him.

Joseph had a dream, and when he told it to his brothers, they hated him all the more. He said to them, "Listen to this dream I had: We were binding sheaves of grain out in the field when suddenly my sheaf rose and stood upright, while your sheaves gathered around mine and bowed down to it."

His brothers said to him, "Do you intend to reign over us? Will you actually rule us?" And they hated him all the more because of his dream and what he had said.

Then he had another dream, and he told it to his

brothers. "Listen," he said, "I had another dream, and this time the sun and moon and eleven stars were bowing down to me."

When he told his father as well as his brothers, his father rebuked him and said, "What is this dream you had? Will your mother and I and your brothers actually come and bow down to the ground before you?" His brothers were jealous of him, but his father kept the matter in mind. (Genesis 37:3–11)

From my chair, it seems obvious that his brothers aren't going to jump all over this dream of his. Even his dad recoiled a bit.

Joseph didn't necessarily do anything wrong here, but he didn't really do anything smart, either. It makes me wonder what his goal was in sharing the dream. If it was to show off, it seems to have backfired. If it was to generate more of a bond between his brothers, who never liked him anyway, that clearly went south as well.

What you say is going to affect people in ways that you may not anticipate. Your words must be considered carefully, your objectives and your audience known intimately. I find it helpful to think through what I want to say and how to say it before it comes out of my mouth, phone, or computer. Words matter . . . delivery of those words, even more so.

Joseph appears to be a bit of a slow learner, given his next interaction with his brothers. His father asked Joseph to check on the brothers out in the fields and bring back a report.

Fine. No big deal, right?

Unfortunately, Joseph has one of the first and worst fashion faux pas in history. He could have just put on something plain to visit the brothers. Instead, he decides to put on the famed coat of many colors his father bestowed to demonstrate his abundant love for his favorite son.

Really? I wish I could have caught Joseph on the way out to the fields and asked if he really thought this was a good idea.

> So Joseph went after his brothers and found them near Dothan. But they saw him in the distance, and before he reached them, they plotted to kill him.
>
> "Here comes that dreamer!" they said to each other. "Come now, let's kill him and throw him into one of these cisterns and say that a ferocious animal devoured him. Then we'll see what comes of his dreams."
>
> When Reuben heard this, he tried to rescue him from their hands. "Let's not take his life," he said. "Don't shed any blood. Throw him into this cistern here in the wilderness, but don't lay a hand on him." Reuben said this to rescue him from them and take him back to his father.
>
> So when Joseph came to his brothers, they stripped him of his robe—the ornate robe he was wearing—and they took him and threw him into the cistern. The cistern was empty; there was no water in it. (Genesis 37:17–24)

Again, Joseph did not mean anything malicious or demeaning. He just demonstrates a lack of common sense and an underdeveloped social intelligence. While the brothers' jealousy was unwarranted and not necessarily his fault, Joseph could have been more aware of rubbing salt into open wounds. Much like when he shared his dreams, this visit ended poorly. In fact, it quickly turned violent. However, the brothers decided it would be more beneficial to sell Joseph than to kill him.

As they sat down to eat their meal, they looked up and saw a caravan of Ishmaelites coming from Gilead. Their camels were loaded with spices, balm and myrrh, and they were on their way to take them down to Egypt.

Judah said to his brothers, "What will we gain if we kill our brother and cover up his blood? Come, let's sell him to the Ishmaelites and not lay our hands on him; after all, he is our brother, our own flesh and blood." His brothers agreed.

So when the Midianite merchants came by, his brothers pulled Joseph up out of the cistern and sold him for twenty shekels of silver to the Ishmaelites, who took him to Egypt. (Genesis 37:25–28)

Operation Visit Brothers in the Field was an epic fail for Joseph. But he's starting to learn. Surely by now he's getting an idea of what kinds of things rub people the wrong way—which is fortunate, since he's now a slave. After his brothers sell him to the Ishmaelites, they in turn sell him to Potiphar, one of Pharaoh's officials.

Much to Joseph's relief, this seems to work out really well.

The LORD was with Joseph so that he prospered, and he lived in the house of his Egyptian master. When his master saw that the LORD was with him and that the LORD gave him success in everything he did, Joseph found favor in his eyes and became his attendant. Potiphar put him in charge of his household, and he entrusted to his care everything he owned. (Genesis 39:2–4)

Joseph was doing so well, in fact, that his master's wife wanted a bit more from Joseph than typical household servants.

My heart always breaks for Joseph while reading this. Potiphar had put him in charge of his entire household. Joseph was a man of integrity and strength and was free from the hatred he grew up around. Things were looking up.

Remember what happens next? Potiphar's wife tries to get Joseph in bed. He refuses; she grabs his cloak when he bolts and then falsely accuses him of attacking her.

Not much chance for recourse there. Once again, though he did nothing wrong, Joseph was punished. Off to jail he went.

At this point, most people, myself included, would be feeling more than a bit bitter. He'd tried so hard to do the right thing his entire life, but everything kept blowing up in his face. I think he'd be justified in at least a little self-pity or cynicism at this point. But here's where Joseph starts teaching the rest of us. Instead of having a cynical or bitter attitude, he maintains a positive tone in his speech and actions—and it pays off.

> But while Joseph was there in the prison, the LORD was with him; he showed him kindness and granted him favor in the eyes of the prison warden. So the warden put Joseph in charge of all those held in the prison, and he was made responsible for all that was done there. The warden paid no attention to anything under Joseph's care, because the LORD was with Joseph and gave him success in whatever he did. (Genesis 39:20–23)

Joseph was consistent. He was a man of character and quality, and his life was much better for it.

Have you ever noticed that Joseph was in a unique kind of prison? The beginning of verse 20 states that he is put in the prison where the king's prisoners were confined. While he was there, his jail mates included the king's cupbearer and baker. One night, those two had dreams.

> "We both had dreams," they answered, "but there is no one to interpret them."
> Then Joseph said to them, "Do not interpretations belong to God? Tell me your dreams." (Genesis 40:8)

They did, and he delivered the meanings: the cupbearer would go back to the king's service and the baker would be executed. Which is exactly what happened. Though Joseph asked the cupbearer to remember him when he returned to the palaces, the cupbearer forgot—for another two years.

Eventually, Pharaoh had a dream too. About cows and corn. Needless to say, he was confused. In his dream, seven sick cows swallowed seven healthy cows and then seven thin heads of grain swallowed seven healthy heads of grain. His armada of wise men and magicians were at a loss. Then, one particular cupbearer happened to remember a promise he had made two years prior to the man in the prison who could interpret dreams.

The cupbearer let Pharaoh know about Joseph and his dream-deciphering gift, and finally, Joseph was summoned from prison to the king's court. One of my favorite details of this story is Joseph's Pharaoh-prep. He shaved and got clean clothes. He was not going to repeat the coat of many colors scenario, in which his carelessness about his appearance incensed his brothers, landed him in a hole, and snowballed from there. This time around, Joseph paid attention to his entire presentation, which no doubt lent him more credibility than had he come in ball and chains.

When he arrived before Pharaoh, Joseph said he personally

couldn't do much of anything for him—instead he extolled the power of God and the divine revelation he had experienced in his life. Joseph allowed God to speak through him and told Pharaoh that the dreams indicated a forthcoming seven years of prosperity, followed by seven years of famine. Joseph advised Pharaoh to put someone in charge of storing away food during the first period of seven so they could survive the next.

Wouldn't you know, as Joseph spelled out the future of Egypt and the kind of leadership that would be necessary to survive, he was inadvertently writing his future job description. Impressed by Joseph's skills and presence, Pharaoh made him second in command over all of Egypt and put the future of the nation in his hands.

This is huge. Of course, it's a major accomplishment for anyone to be appointed to this type of job. But Joseph just came directly from prison! He hadn't been out on parole. He wasn't making an appeal. He went from inmate to running the country. Given the Egyptian dynasty at that point in history, it would be more accurate to say he was running the most powerful country in the world.

Not bad for a kid whose brothers sold him, a man whose employer's wife framed him, and an inmate whose friend had forgotten him for two years. What's even more remarkable about this is that Pharaoh appointed him recognizing that his wisdom was from God. Egypt was not a monotheistic nation, by any means. They worshipped multiple gods but had never worshipped the God of Israel.

Joseph knew that as well. He took a risk by saying that he couldn't interpret Pharaoh's dream on his own, but only through God's power. Joseph didn't circumvent the source of his wisdom, nor did he attempt to hoodwink the most power-ful man in the world. Rather, he provided a service to Pharaoh with excellence and full acknowledgment that it was indeed a service that could only be provided through and with God.

Today, most Christians are either afraid to admit their faith in a very secular landscape or don't pay enough attention to the rest of the world so as to present Christ with excellence. In so many ways, we have diminished the concept of Christianity to a list of right and wrong. If something falls in the wrong column, we do all we can to distance ourselves (at least in public). In the process, we insulate and isolate and fall completely out of touch with the rest of society. It's impossible to present a compelling case for anything to a group of people you know nothing about.

When we represent God in a tone or manner that undermines His greatness, we represent Him incorrectly and can turn other people off of this whole notion of Christianity. Much like a song delivered as a string of notes disconnected from emotion, a Christian life of going through the motions lacks conviction, passion, and charisma. Everything you do matters to someone. Someone will have their eyes on you—at church as well as at home, at work, at the gym, and on the Internet. What are they going to see? You have more influence than you realize. Don't squander it.

Joseph was smart in learning his audience and recasting his presentation to be compelling and effective. Learning from prior mistakes, he developed his voice to have a tone and texture that could be heard. Then when he had the people's attention, he pointed them directly to the source of his knowledge.

Joseph's appointment isn't the end of his story. The famine he had predicted happened and people were coming from all over to Egypt to get the food he had helped store. His brothers just so happened to be among the hungry.

When we meet them again, they're a different group of

men, for sure. Their father had been wrecked when Joseph disappeared. Seeing the consequences of their jealousy and anger, they became kinder, more compassionate, and overall better people.

Joseph knew it. He recognized them immediately, although they didn't know who he was. So Joseph tested them—not to be cruel, but to see the kind of men his brothers had become. He wanted to see if they protected each other or disregarded their family the way they had disregarded him.

He kept up the farce for a while. The whole time, he maintained a tone of aloofness, never once letting on his true identity. Even so, he could see that they were different. They were warm. They exuded genuine compassion, concern, fear, regret, and protectiveness. Their hearts were right. Without agenda or even awareness, the brothers' overall demeanor was so improved that Joseph, whom they had nearly murdered, forgave them as well.

The most profound, emotional moment of this roller-coaster story comes when Joseph finally reveals himself to his brothers.

> Then Joseph could no longer control himself before all his attendants, and he cried out, "Have everyone leave my presence!" So there was no one with Joseph when he made himself known to his brothers. And he wept so loudly that the Egyptians heard him, and Pharaoh's household heard about it.
>
> Joseph said to his brothers, "I am Joseph! Is my father still living?" But his brothers were not able to answer him, because they were terrified at his presence.
>
> Then Joseph said to his brothers, "Come close to me." When they had done so, he said, "I am your brother

Joseph, the one you sold into Egypt! And now, do not be distressed and do not be angry with yourselves for selling me here, because it was to save lives that God sent me ahead of you. For two years now there has been famine in the land, and for the next five years there will be no plowing and reaping. But God sent me ahead of you to preserve for you a remnant on earth and to save your lives by a great deliverance." (Genesis 45:1–7)

If ever there was a person justified in their bitterness, it was Joseph. But he doesn't go there. His tone is one of gratitude, kindness, and reconciliation.

Does the tone of your voice, the tone of your life, reflect things that are good? Is it inviting, or does it turn people away? Do you encourage or discourage with the way you express yourself? Are you representing Christ in a manner that will draw people to Him or push them away?

Authentic delivery will make or break a friendship or relationship. It's easy to spend your entire life hiding from intimacy. Computers, phones, schedules, significant others, addictions—these can be convenient shelters that extract you from the world and those around you. Over time, you may very well forget how to interact with people in a way that's life-giving for both of you.

When I'm singing, I want people to feel something. I want my tone to resonate with the message of the song and the texture of my voice to emote its passion. I want to stand out from the crowd because my voice is distinct and memorable. Adele didn't win all those Grammys because she has a several octave range. She won because she took time to care about how she delivered every note she sang or played. It touched people and stayed with them.

Every conversation you have has the potential to do the same. If—that's a big *if*—your objective is about loving others.

Your voice and your life is bigger than you. You create experiences for everyone you meet—positive or negative, conscious or unconscious. To find your true voice, passion, and purpose in life, you absolutely must realize that it will NOT be about you. God didn't create us to serve ourselves; He created us for His glory, which is evident when we love, serve, and care for others.

The quality of your voice and your life will either draw people in or repel them. I can probably guess which one you prefer. Just bear in mind that effective tone and texture don't just happen. You have to observe, work for, practice, and intentionally harness that sincerity.

Drink deep from the well of emotions your Creator has placed within you—and pass the cup.

Chapter 8

WORKING THE STAGE: ENGAGE, CONNECT, GROW

I recorded my first album in 1999. It was a pre-Facebook, pre-Twitter, pre-Instagram world. As a performer, you had essentially two mediums by which to reach your audience—your recorded music and your live show. Performance was key, and I quickly learned how to deliver. I could go out and impress everyone with the high notes. I could work that stage.

But there was something missing. There was a deeper connection to be had, but I couldn't quite get there. I was singing great songs, but they were great songs others had written. They had come from other people's life experiences and other people's hearts and, though they were brilliant, they weren't authentically me. It was at that point that I decided to begin the risky business of writing my own songs.

I began taking my struggles, my relationship with the Lord, my insecurities and fears and turned them into songs. At the same time, I was learning how to be honest, transparent and authentic with my audience. This allowed me to own the stage in a much deeper way. I was no longer just a singer, and the audience was no longer made up of just fans. We were becoming friends.

Different people do it in different ways, but I decided that letting people into my story was the best way for me to connect with the audience and with myself. Today, every time I go on stage, I sense a genuine heart-to-heart connection. I feel like the audience knows me, and watching them react to my songs helps me know them.

The same is true with social media. Unlike the beginning of my career, in which concerts and radio were about the extent of your reach, Twitter, Facebook, Instagram and the like are as much a part of my platform and stage, so to speak, as any concert hall. I decided long ago that I could have someone else post for me or I could do it myself. I wanted to be open and transparent and, for better or for worse, it has changed my platform and helped me develop deeper relationships than I ever thought possible.

Of course, there are risks to being an open book. It can lead to criticism and misinterpretation of events. Case in point: the Grammys. I didn't walk out. I left early. Social media turned it into something it wasn't, but you have to take the bad with the good. I've found over and over that the reward of being authentic on any stage is so much greater than the risk of being hurt.

The Bible is full of public personas who took various "stages" throughout their lives and ministry. Consider Elijah, Moses, Daniel, Deborah, Isaiah and Paul, Mary, the Samaritan woman at the well. These passionate orators felt driven to deliver the message God had placed within them. The greatest of all time, however, is Jesus. He not only effectively works every stage He encounters but also selects those stages meticulously and then surrenders them immediately into the hands of His Father. His ministry is the ultimate model of one who connects with, creates an experience for, and retains an audience.

Looking closely at His methodology, these tactics leap off the pages of the Bible and translate to those seeking and working a crowd in the twenty-first century.

- Master your message.
- See people, not circumstances.
- Speak the language of your audience.
- Value your audience consistently.

In some way, we're all on a stage every single day. Whether you stay at home with your children, run a nonprofit, work in a corporate setting, or minister to a congregation, your surroundings are your stage. If you are to make the most of it, those same strategies apply.

Even if they seem uncomfortable . . .

It's one thing to find your voice. But it's not worth much if you never use it. Don't let a lack of confidence or motivation steal your stage.

KNOWLEDGE BREEDS CONFIDENCE

*E*arlier, we visited the story of Jesus and His time of temptation in the wilderness. Let's pick up that story. Immediately following the desert trials, Jesus returns home. He wastes no time in assuming His role as a teacher and Rabbi. Things start out well, but then Jesus hits a roadblock.

Jesus returned to Galilee in the power of the Spirit, and news about him spread through the whole countryside. He was teaching in their synagogues, and everyone praised him. . . .

"Truly I tell you," he continued, "no prophet is accepted in his hometown. I assure you that there were many widows in Israel in Elijah's time, when the sky was shut for three and a half years and there was a severe famine throughout the land. Yet Elijah was not sent to any of them, but to a widow in Zarephath in the region of Sidon. And there were many in Israel with leprosy in the time of Elisha the prophet, yet not one of them was cleansed—only Naaman the Syrian."

All the people in the synagogue were furious when they heard this. They got up, drove him out of the town, and took him to the brow of the hill on which the town was built, in order to throw him off the cliff. But he walked right through the crowd and went on his way. Then he went down to Capernaum, a town in Galilee, and on the Sabbath he taught the people. They were amazed at his teaching, because his words had authority. (Luke 4:14–15, 24–32)

Wow! There is so much here. Right before this passage, we see Jesus using Scripture to combat temptation. He clearly has an authoritative grasp on Scripture, which He immediately puts to use, heading straight for the synagogue. The text speaks for itself—they loved Him!

And then He goes home.

This is likely a scenario that has played out countless times. I'm sure many people return from college or from their first venture into the "real world" and have wonderful experiences with loving and supporting hometowns and families. I'm equally sure many people go home to nothing but dashed expectations and disappointment. Talk about a blow! Here you are on your own for the first time. Even if you're fortunate enough to have made a clean dive into your adult life . . . it's hard! When you go home feeling that your salary still isn't impressive enough or your family doesn't revere you like your sorority sisters or your coworkers did, it's enough to crush your spirit or at least to send you diving under the covers with a pint of Ben & Jerry's. Swallowing rejection from home is difficult. Even more so experiencing disappointment when you are not respected in the field you've committed your life and career to!

Jesus hadn't been out in the desert for fun. He was doing intense work and battle. He was refining and sharpening and priming to go change the world.

But when He went back home, the door was slammed in His face.

And what did He do? "He walked right through the crowd and went on his way" (Luke 4:30).

Wouldn't you love to have that sense of confidence? To be so sure of yourself and what you were investing your life in that you could hold your head high and move on even when rejected by those closest to you? I'd *love* to be that sure of myself!

The great thing is, we can be! Jesus didn't hold His head high and move on for His sake. He was showing us how to handle the haters: rise above and move along. He goes on to demonstrate the results of such confidence: "Then he went down to Capernaum, a town in Galilee, and on the Sabbath he taught the people. They were amazed at his teaching, because his words had authority" (Luke 4:31–32).

What a satisfying moment! I know Jesus was much more humble and gracious than I would have been. The lesson here is so clear. Know who you are and what you are about, and it doesn't matter what crowd boos you off; there is another waiting to welcome you and drink in your message, your talent, your gifts . . . you!

A performer has to have confidence to even begin working a stage. You develop this self-assurance through proper preparation and, most importantly, a solid foundation of knowing who you are in Christ. Without it, your career will be short lived.

You have to have that same level of confidence in your life. God has given you a unique voice, role, and responsibility. But you have to know your material and know how to deliver if you're ever to exhibit the confidence that won't be shaken when people turn away. Know who you are. Trust who you are. And then, take that stage by storm.

SEE PEOPLE, NOT CIRCUMSTANCES

*T*here have been many a show date when I would have been much happier to crawl in bed, take a nap, read a book, or just put my feet up for a while. On those days, the circumstances urge me to take it easy. However, when I think about the people who will be in that audience, the lives that God has been preparing to bless through my music, it fortifies my resolve to not dwell on circumstances but to look past myself and see others. It's only then that I can be to others what God created me to be. In other words, God has prepared my stage just like He has prepared yours. And it is His desire that the show—your show, my show—must go on.

I can think of many times when Jesus embraced that very idea, not allowing the circumstances to dictate where and when He would speak. We see this at work in the feeding of the five thousand.

> When Jesus landed and saw a large crowd, he had compassion on them, because they were like sheep

without a shepherd. So he began teaching them many things.

By this time it was late in the day, so his disciples came to him. "This is a remote place," they said, "and it's already very late. Send the people away so that they can go to the surrounding countryside and villages and buy themselves something to eat."

But he answered, "You give them something to eat." (Mark 6:34–37)

Can you imagine the disciples' alarm at this moment? Jesus is asking the impossible here, and they know it.

They said to him, "That would take more than half a year's wages! Are we to go and spend that much on bread and give it to them to eat?"

"How many loaves do you have?" he asked. "Go and see."

When they found out, they said, "Five—and two fish."

Then Jesus directed them to have all the people sit down in groups on the green grass. So they sat down in groups of hundreds and fifties. Taking the five loaves and the two fish and looking up to heaven, he gave thanks and broke the loaves. Then he gave them to his disciples to distribute to the people. He also divided the two fish among them all. They all ate and were satisfied, and the disciples picked up twelve basketfuls of broken pieces of bread and fish. The number of the men who had eaten was five thousand. (Mark 6:37–44)

The disciples make me think of the band members who'd rather cancel than carry on. And who blames them? This was a mess! The timing wasn't good. It was close to meal time. Clearly, the location was a challenge. On top of all that, people were hungry and there was nothing to eat! To me, it makes sense to cancel the show—it's just a logistical nightmare. But how often do we need to be reminded that God isn't bound by logistics?

He wasn't about to send anyone away. I do find his disciples' response to Him quite funny. "They said to him, 'That would take more than half a year's wages! Are we to go and spend that much on bread and give it to them to eat?'" (Mark 6:37).

How much more do they have to see to get it? They are using this as an excuse—a seemingly legitimate excuse—to move on from a group of people. The cost is worth more than the benefit, from a natural perspective. And that's precisely the point. God doesn't have a worldly perspective, but an eternal one that we can't really grasp yet. And that's okay. We just have to do what the disciples did next: gather what we have and show up.

I love when the Bible mirrors things in my life. As a mom, I'm always thinking of where my kids are, where they need to be, and if they've eaten. It's somewhat comforting to see the men who traveled and lived and worked with Jesus freak out about dinner, because that's me every day!

This scenario shows me so much about God's character and the ways that He cares for us. First, when He arrives on the scene, He doesn't question the people about why they're there or what they're doing. He sees that they look lost and starts teaching. There's no preface. There's no reprimand. There's a need and He has the answer.

Second, He knew what time of day it was. Aware that people would be hungry soon, He doesn't hesitate in asking His disciples to feed everyone. He doesn't form a catering committee. He doesn't ask if any of the twelve have cooking abilities. He simply sees the need, sees His workers, and asks them to meet the need—to gather what they have and give it to Him. He made it all work.

Jesus saw an opportunity to teach and to bless a huge crowd of people. He didn't let the circumstances steal that stage or the naysayers force Him to call it quits.

In our lives, how often do we walk away from people who may need to hear from us because it's inconvenient? Or because we don't feel like we have anything to offer? For me, that's way too often . . . and I'm not referring to my life as an artist. As a wife, a mom, a friend, a sister, a daughter, I'm given the opportunity to take the stage and offer part of myself to someone every day. We all are. It's time to drop the excuses and stop letting our circumstances dictate our stage time.

SPEAK THE LANGUAGE OF YOUR AUDIENCE

A quick glance through the Gospels relates parable after illustration after story from the lips of Jesus. No matter how lofty the concept, He had a gift for speaking to people where they were, using language and illustrations that were relevant to them.

He spoke to farmers:

> "No good tree bears bad fruit, nor does a bad tree bear good fruit. Each tree is recognized by its own fruit. People do not pick figs from thorn bushes, or grapes from briers. A good man brings good things out of the good stored up in his heart, and an evil man brings evil things out of the evil stored up in his heart. For the mouth speaks what the heart is full of." (Luke 6:43–45)

He spoke to carpenters:

> "Why do you call me, 'Lord, Lord,' and do not do what I say? As for everyone who comes to me and hears my words and puts them into practice, I will show you what they are like. They are like a man building a house, who dug down deep and laid the foundation on rock. When a flood came, the torrent struck that house but could not shake it, because it was well built. But the one who hears my words and does not put them into practice is like a man who built a house on the ground without a foundation. The moment the torrent struck that house, it collapsed and its destruction was complete." (Luke 6:46–49)

He spoke to fishermen:

> "Once again, the kingdom of heaven is like a net that was let down into the lake and caught all kinds of fish. When it was full, the fishermen pulled it up on the shore. Then they sat down and collected the good fish in baskets, but threw the bad away. This is how it will be at the end of the age. The angels will come and separate the wicked from the righteous." (Matthew 13:47–49)

He paid attention to the people around Him and chose His words very carefully. He connected with them. Never condescending, never self-absorbed, His presentation was always sincere and accessible.

If I'm singing to a group of women at a weekend conference, I will fashion my presentation differently than an arena performance. If I don't adjust my presentation to the audience in front of me, I'll miss them.

When you have an opportunity to take your stage—at home, work, church, wherever—your message will get nowhere if you're not paying attention to the language of whoever you may be trying to reach.

This isn't necessarily easy to do. It requires humility. It cannot be about you and your intelligence, skills, and capacity to impress. Your interaction, opportunity, performance must be oriented toward others or you'll be playing to an empty room.

Aim to Serve Your Audience

One of the most distinct and appealing characteristics of Jesus' presentation is the absence of pretense and abundance of inclusion.

In Jesus' day, Jews didn't consort with Romans or Samaritans or many other people groups. Jesus did. Religious leaders didn't hang around with tax collectors or prostitutes. Jesus did. His mission and message were never confined to a certain people group. He healed the servant of a humble Gentile centurion (Luke 7:1–10). He welcomed little children, "for the kingdom of heaven belongs to such as these" (Matthew 19:14). Much to the chagrin of teachers of the law, he healed a paralyzed man and publicly pronounced him forgiven (Matthew 9:1–8). Add better-known names like Zacchaeus, Nicodemus, Mary Magdalene, and Matthew to that long list of people Jesus shouldn't have been associated with. All of them were on the outskirts of His culture of origin by fault or default, yet Jesus worked His way onto their stage.

No matter how many times the disciples questioned Him or the Pharisees berated Him, Jesus let nothing prevent Him from getting his point across. More likely than not, He considered the various factions that would be represented in the crowds who heard His teachings and had different intentions for each of them. He knew when He wanted to provoke the Pharisees or humble His disciples. Jesus didn't do anything on a whim. He included those who loved and agreed with Him as well as those who opposed Him.

Do you ever avoid certain people just because? Did your upbringing consciously or unconsciously impact the way you view and interact with others? It is so easy to get lost in the familiar, never straying beyond. In doing so, though, we're sabotaging our own quality of life and an opportunity to learn, minister, and build relationships.

If there were ever a social etiquette lesson to learn from Jesus, it is to engage everyone, stop making assumptions, and avoid segregation like a plague.

Jesus wasn't there just to save folks like the disciples (who were quite a diverse bunch of their own). His love is so much bigger than that. He came to save all of us—not just the ones who show up at the right church on Sunday morning. His words—and ultimately His blood—vanquished a barrier between God and humanity.

No matter how down or worthless you may feel, no matter how culture has attempted to box you in and cut you off, remind yourself of what a prize you are to Him. You are worth dying for. Once you realize that, you'll start to understand that everyone is worth dying for in Jesus' eyes.

Work Your Crowd

As I mentioned at the very beginning of this book, indeed, all the world is a stage. Are you working yours? Are you engaging those who you serve in the best way you can?

Be honest with yourself. Pray about this. Seek to have an open mind and an open heart.

When you do, your impact on this world will explode.

You've got a voice, you've got a stage . . . Now it's time do the work.

Start with your audience. Observe the people around you. What do they need? What resonates with them? Whom have you left out? Are there any fears in your life that are holding you back?

Whatever stands in your way of sharing your voice confidently and with conviction, identify it; write it down if you need to. Bring it into focus and prayerfully, diligently walk with God towards a resolution. He gave you your platform and He will equip you with all you need to make the most of it.

Chapter 9

BEAUTY IN THE BREAKING

---

*R*emember that time I was about to perform at the Ryman Auditorium with Wynonna Judd? There's more to the story.

The truth is, when the doctor told me I had a less than 3 percent chance of having children, the bottom fell out of my world. That's not the best time to waltz out into the spotlight and give your all to a packed out legacy concert hall.

I was broken. The last thing I felt like doing was taking the stage to sing a song about how God works all things together for good. It so happened that was exactly the song Wynonna and I had worked on together, but I was rehearsing a different song in my head: "You're never going to be a mother. You're *never* going to be a mother."

I was a mess and trying to hold myself together backstage. At that moment, I thought nothing good could possibly arise from my situation.

My manager looked me straight in the eye and said, "If you believe the words in the song you're about to sing, I need you to get on that stage."

I wasn't sure if I did believe it, but I wanted to. I had rehearsed this song with the wild hope that it would encourage my listeners, that they would know just how much God loves and cares for them even in the middle of their worst nightmare.

It was time. I walked out onto the stage with Wynonna, we gave it our all, and the song I hoped would encourage others ended up being my lifeline that night. I sang the words I most needed to hear, the words I most needed to believe.

But let me tell you something: It still hurt. And I would hurt for a long time.

I've often wondered why pain has to be such an integral part of life. After all, God created the universe. Why do we have to hurt so much just to be a part of it? Disappointment, illness, loss, grief come to all of us. Some seem to have to bear more than others, but no one is immune to problems. Even God, in all His graciousness, promises that "In this world you will have trouble." But, He goes on: "Take heart! I have overcome the world" (John 16:33).

The fears my husband and I had tried to drown out the truth—that God is ultimately in control, that He can move mountains, split oceans, and make babies. Still, we put on the bravest faces we could and moved ahead with IVF treatments. I don't believe you can separate God and science. I think He uses modern science for the good of those who love Him. I resolved with God that if it were His will, I would trust Him no matter what. Even so, I was terrified that it wasn't going to go in our favor, right up to the day we were to find out if the treatment worked.

Miraculously, the treatment was a success, and we conceived—twins! Even more astounding, it wasn't long after their birth that we got pregnant with our third daughter. She was our little miracle we didn't know we needed. Upon learning the news, I sobbed like a baby, thanked God that He would bless us so, and offered apologies for my doubt.

I learned something during this season: Our hurt is not our own. In fact, Jesus Christ bore the agony of mankind. In Isaiah, it's foretold that He would suffer. "He was despised and rejected by mankind, a man of suffering, and familiar with pain" (Isaiah 53:3).

I still find myself asking, Why? Is the pain that necessary?

And then I remember that pain is not God's choice. Pain is often a result of human choices . . . choices that He has given us out of His grace and mercy. He's not a God of coercion or force. He allows us to freely come or freely go. But the fallout remains. And whether we are His or not, we still crawl through this life in the trenches dug by those who trudged through before us.

That's not to say that life is doom and gloom and we should just accept it. Rather, life is a wealth of beauty hidden in the brokenness.

CATCH A BREAK

*W*hen you're singing, your voice has a natural break. Usually, it's when you transition from chest voice—a deep, lower resonance—to head voice—a higher, often thinner tone. If unintentional, a break in your voice can be embarrassing and completely not what you were going for in a performance. However, when anticipated, a vocal break can become one of the most interesting and beautiful moments in a song. It's where the texture of your voice pushes through. It's a moment of vulnerability when emotion can take the spotlight. Suddenly, a vocal break is no longer a detriment; it's an element of beauty.

I don't think God causes the struggle and pain in our lives. I do believe, though, that there will always be a lesson to emerge from whatever pain comes along. Let's go back to Peter, those terrified disciples, and that unrelenting storm. The story in Matthew clearly delivers the message of faith, doubt, fear, and our willingness to get out of the boat. But there's more. This story isn't just a lesson; it reveals a sacred and precious image of the nature of God and the lengths He will go to in order to humble us, teach us, and love us; and it begins to take shape long before anyone sets a foot on that boat.

If you recall, the story begins on a mountaintop. Jesus had just finished preaching to throngs of people and sent the disciples ahead while He stayed on the mountain to pray. He didn't mention anything about the weather. He didn't advise them to keep an eye on the sky. He simply told them to go. In His omnipotence, He knew a storm was on the horizon, and He sent them directly into it.

When I ponder that, I can't help but question His teaching method. At the same time, I know He doesn't make mistakes nor does He do anything without intention. He sent them where they needed to be. I don't think His end goal had anything to do with causing them pain or scaring them. I think He sent them to the place where they could learn the most—not a mountaintop, but a stormy sea.

I think He does the same for you and me today. Just as He did for the disciples, He does what He needs to do to humble us, teach us, and love us. While we're in the midst of the maelstrom, getting tossed around by waves that rage all around us, it's pretty natural to feel helpless and scared and unequipped. I've been there many times and have often been ashamed at my own lack of faith and my fear. Sometimes, I don't even feel eligible to lead or influence others, but the Bible tells us that in our weakness, His strength is made perfect. It is when we are broken that Jesus does His best work.

I know these statements may seem trite, but my intent is not to speak flippantly about the pain and brokenness we experience in life. It helps me to trust God and have faith that He has an outcome greater than the moment of brokenness, even if not revealed in this life. My confidence comes from Scripture. Over and over, we read of men and women who are battered and bruised and worn down in ways that would devastate most anyone. Yet over and over, we see God redeem their story.

Naomi and Ruth, Job, Moses . . . heroes of the faith. Generations know their names and their stories. Their pains and their outcomes were vastly different but all significant. When I am in the depths, I find comfort in their stories and their pain because I know that God used their brokenness for more. Generations later, their losses are helping me and so many others. Even if they never knew the beauty God fashioned from their shattered pieces, if nothing more ever came of their pain, that would be enough. It's His story. He knows the end and He loves you and He will never toss aside your fragments.

You just have to be willing to trust Him with every splintered piece of your bruised and broken heart. Much like singing, where any number of things can cause your voice to crack or break—fatigue, overuse, illness—brokenness can come from many places and leave any number of scars—bitterness, grief, fear, or shame.

No matter the origin or the outcome, He is more than able to put us back together.

BROKEN AND BITTER

*T*he story of Naomi and Ruth is one of the most beautiful and compelling in Scripture. Typically, we focus on Ruth and her eventual marriage to Boaz, her kinsmen redeemer. It was customary in those days for a family member to marry the widow of another member of the family. But I find even greater hope when I see Ruth's mother-in-law, Naomi, weather her staggering loss and experience the redemption that eventually played out.

> Now Elimelek, Naomi's husband, died, and she was left with her two sons. They married Moabite women, one named Orpah and the other Ruth. After they had lived there about ten years, both Mahlon and Kilion also died, and Naomi was left without her two sons and her husband. . . .
>
> "Don't call me Naomi," she told them. "Call me Mara, because the Almighty has made my life very bitter. I went away full, but the LORD has brought me back empty. Why call me Naomi? The LORD has afflicted me; the Almighty has brought misfortune upon me." (Ruth 1:3–5, 20–21)

I learned this story when I was a child. Now that I am a mother, though, the story carries an intense, almost revelatory degree of pain. Within a decade, Naomi became a widow and buried her two sons. I hope I can never fully identify with her. Just thinking about it makes me physically ill. If you're a wife or mom, there may be no greater loss or pain.

"I went away full, but the Lord has brought me back empty."

I think empty is far too gentle a word. Gutted, destroyed, devastated . . . that's where I would be so tempted to dwell. Then again, if I had a daughter-in-law like Ruth, I think I could find the strength to keep going.

Ruth, also a widow, is fiercely loyal to Naomi. She is willing to abandon the only life she had ever known in order to stay with, comfort, protect, and nurture her mother-in-law. When they return to Bethlehem together, they eventually find renewed life. Ruth remarries; Naomi receives the unexpected blessing of a grandchild. The pain of their broken lives begins to heal, and through the birth of that child, they become a part of the greatest lineage the world has ever known.

> Then Naomi took the child in her arms and cared for
> him. The women living there said, "Naomi has a son!"
> And they named him Obed. He was the father of Jesse,
> the father of David. (Ruth 4:16–17)

There are two genealogies of Jesus in Scripture—one in Matthew and one in Luke. While they differ from each other significantly, both show that Jesus descended from the line of David. It is Matthew's account that names women—non-Jewish mothers even—including Ruth.

There's a striking irony here . . . Because Naomi lost her sons, she and Ruth returned to Bethlehem and built a new life from the pain . . . a new life that would play a part in the plan that God had from the beginning: sending His Son, Jesus, to His death. A death that would ensure new life for all.

God redeemed Naomi's brokenness and assuaged her bitterness. God hadn't abandoned her story or her heart. He took her hand and walked through the mire with her. And the story carried on.

SHAMED AND REJECTED

*W*hile Moses is most often associated with the emancipation of the Hebrews from Pharaoh's rule, his early life belied defeat rather than victory for many years. Most people know the story of Moses' mother placing him in a basket on the Nile in an attempt to save his life. Pharaoh's sister found him and raised him within the Egyptian dynasty.

When Moses learned of his origin several years later, things quickly spiraled downward. Witnessing with new eyes the horrendous oppression of the Hebrew nation at the hand of Egypt, he rose up to oppose it.

> One day, after Moses had grown up, he went out to where his own people were and watched them at their hard labor. He saw an Egyptian beating a Hebrew, one of his own people. Looking this way and that and seeing no one, he killed the Egyptian and hid him in the sand. The next day he went out and saw two Hebrews fighting. He asked the one in the wrong, "Why are you hitting your fellow Hebrew?"
>
> The man said, "Who made you ruler and judge over us? Are you thinking of killing me as you killed the Egyptian?" Then Moses was afraid and thought, "What I did must have become known." (Exodus 2:11–14)

He was right. Banished from the only home he'd ever known, the family he thought was his own cut him out completely, yet he was not accepted by his people.

I struggle so much with a fear of rejection, among other things. I would probably have come undone if my family kicked me out. However, the ink was not yet dry on his story.

Moses went to Midian, where he started a new life. He got married, had a child, and was content with the hand he had been dealt.

God wasn't.

In His perfect timing and way, God called Moses to the burning bush.

> Now Moses was tending the flock of Jethro his father-in-law, the priest of Midian, and he led the flock to the far side of the wilderness and came to Horeb, the mountain of God. There the angel of the LORD appeared to him in flames of fire from within a bush. Moses saw that though the bush was on fire it did not burn up. So Moses thought, "I will go over and see this strange sight—why the bush does not burn up."
>
> When the LORD saw that he had gone over to look, God called to him from within the bush, "Moses! Moses!" (Exodus 3:1–4)

He had Moses' attention and filled him in on the rest of the story. He was to return to Egypt and free God's people.

God asked Moses to go back to where he had been wanted for murder, the place from which his family expelled him. I can't imagine a place I'd like more to avoid. That probably played into Moses' response . . .

> Moses said to the LORD, "Pardon your servant, Lord. I have never been eloquent, neither in the past nor since you have spoken to your servant. I am slow of speech and tongue."
>
> The LORD said to him, "Who gave human beings their

mouths? Who makes them deaf or mute? Who gives them sight or makes them blind? Is it not I, the LORD? Now go; I will help you speak and will teach you what to say."

But Moses said, "Pardon your servant, Lord. Please send someone else."

Then the LORD's anger burned against Moses and he said, "What about your brother, Aaron the Levite? I know he can speak well. He is already on his way to meet you, and he will be glad to see you. You shall speak to him and put words in his mouth; I will help both of you speak and will teach you what to do. He will speak to the people for you, and it will be as if he were your mouth and as if you were God to him. But take this staff in your hand so you can perform the signs with it." (Exodus 4:10–17)

Moses was afraid that if he spoke, his voice would break. In fact, he himself was in a broken place. But God sent him to face it. When you think about it, the strategy here seems backwards. You'd think that it would be more advantageous to have someone on the inside. Common sense says that a Moses that Pharaoh likes and considers family would get a lot further than Moses the reject wanted for murder.

In fact, I completely believe that Moses could have gotten miles farther with the Egyptian monarchy had he still been a part of it. God chose to humble and prepare Moses in a unique way during his brokenness and exile. He didn't need Moses to keep things together for Him. He decided to allow Moses to be His mouthpiece after he had been broken. Through the tattered remnants of Moses' life, God could shine through. Moses' rejection and shame created within him a humility that allowed him to step aside and let God be God—the ultimate victor . . . the deliverer.

UNSPEAKABLE LOSS

*T*he story of Job plays out like a heartbreaking movie. The circumstance and the losses he endured were staggering beyond comprehension. In the span of a few days, his children were killed, his property destroyed, and his servants slaughtered. After that, he got sick . . . boils and blisters all over his body. It's shocking to picture. Even more so, however, is his response.

> At this, Job got up and tore his robe and shaved his head. Then he fell to the ground in worship and said:
>
> *"Naked I came from my mother's womb,*
> *and naked I will depart.*
> *The LORD gave and the LORD has taken away;*
> *may the name of the LORD be praised."*
>
> In all this, Job did not sin by charging God with wrongdoing. (Job 1:20–22)

Look at the second part of verse 20. Worship. Job's first response is worship.

Accepting trouble instead of good is hard. I really don't understand how he could take such a position in light of what had happened. On top of it all, his friends and his wife assumed Job must have done something terrible for God to allow all this pain. For nearly forty chapters, we see a volley between Job and his friends and family. Nineteen chapters in, Job is still extolling his redeemer!

> *"Oh, that my words were recorded,*
> *that they were written on a scroll,*

> *that they were inscribed with an iron tool on lead,*
> *or engraved in rock forever!*
> *I know that my redeemer lives,*
> *and that in the end he will stand on the earth.*
> *And after my skin has been destroyed,*
> *yet in my flesh I will see God;*
> *I myself will see him*
> *with my own eyes—I, and not another.*
> *How my heart yearns within me! (Job 19:23–27)*

Despite everything, Job stands firm. Broken, but so grounded in the truth and love of God, even here, he doesn't blame God. He can't wait to see Him!

To be honest, I've blamed God for much smaller things than what Job was facing. His faith blows me away. It's not that he understands the circumstances and the trials. Rather, he recognizes the sovereignty of God and even when he has nothing left, he doesn't let go.

> *Where then does wisdom come from?*
> *Where does understanding dwell?*
> *It is hidden from the eyes of every living thing,*
> *concealed even from the birds in the sky.*
> *Destruction and Death say,*
> *"Only a rumor of it has reached our ears."*
> *God understands the way to it*
> *and he alone knows where it dwells,*
> *for he views the ends of the earth*
> *and sees everything under the heavens.*
> *When he established the force of the wind*
> *and measured out the waters,*
> *when he made a decree for the rain*

> *and a path for the thunderstorm,*
> *then he looked at wisdom and appraised it;*
> *he confirmed it and tested it.*
> *And he said to the human race,*
> *"The fear of the* LORD—*that is wisdom,*
> *and to shun evil is understanding." (Job 28:20–28)*

There are so many tragedies and losses that make no sense at all. You can't see God in any of it.

My mind goes to Sandy Hook. I bet you remember where you were when you learned of this atrocity. I'm sure your heart, like mine, was broken at this staggering, senseless, heinous act.

On December 14, 2012, Adam Lanza shot and killed twenty children and six adults at an elementary school. I can't even put this on paper today without crying. The magnitude of that tragedy is unbearable.

I think of my three precious girls. They go to school. The idea that I'd drop them off one morning and never see them again is incomprehensible. In those moments, I feel paralyzed. I want to believe God's sovereignty. I want to trust His plan, but I can't conceive of something good coming from the execution of twenty children. It's the kind of tragedy that never should make sense. I don't want to be able to rationalize something like that. All I can do is keep breathing. Sit among the broken shards until He reveals Himself.

When Job lost everything, he still knew that God was bigger and that somehow the most excruciating circumstances were part of a story he couldn't yet understand.

> After Job had prayed for his friends, the LORD restored his fortunes and gave him twice as much as he had before. All his brothers and sisters and everyone

who had known him before came and ate with him in his house. They comforted and consoled him over all the trouble the LORD had brought on him, and each one gave him a piece of silver and a gold ring.

The LORD blessed the latter part of Job's life more than the former part. He had fourteen thousand sheep, six thousand camels, a thousand yoke of oxen and a thousand donkeys. And he also had seven sons and three daughters. The first daughter he named Jemimah, the second Keziah and the third Keren-Happuch. Nowhere in all the land were there found women as beautiful as Job's daughters, and their father granted them an inheritance along with their brothers.

After this, Job lived a hundred and forty years; he saw his children and their children to the fourth generation. And so Job died, an old man and full of years. (Job 42:10–17)

Your story isn't finished. Your brokenness doesn't define your life. The One who penned the universe does.

Your faith will be tested, and you will find yourself in turmoil, at times, not understanding, knowing, or seeing.

But even when your voice is broken, God still hears it. He may not fix the break or take away the pain, but He won't leave you to sit in it alone. Naomi and Moses and Job suffered. They were broken. But eventually, in God's timing and in God's way, He restored them and rewarded their faithfulness. He longs to do the same for you and for me.

In my darkest moments, when my heart is torn from my chest and I feel destroyed, all I can do is know that God is love—and love is holding me.

Chapter 10

FINDING YOUR SONG

გა

I've sung a lot of songs in my career. I am blessed to be married to one of the greatest songwriters in the world and have been surrounded by incredibly talented songwriters throughout the years, all of whom have impacted my own songwriting.

From this bevy of writers, a wealth of music has come forth. Every song I've recorded, I'm proud of. Each has something to say and reflects a moment of inspiration.

Looking back over the years, however, I can see a distinct progression in my song selection, with a major shift occurring around 2005.

That was the year that I founded Abolition International (now known as Hope for Justice) and jumped into the fight against human trafficking after my eyes were opened in India to the reality these women should never have to live. It was also the year I released the album, *Awaken*. From the title through the last song, the entire album was so representative of that period of my life and the awakening I was experiencing as a Christian, as a wife, as a woman, as one who could change the world.

That was the year I truly found my voice. God expected more from me than background music. He gave me an instrument that could touch and challenge hearts. He gave me the capacity to not only see pain and beauty in life but to assuage pain and create beauty.

My eyes were opened to the importance of using my voice in significant ways. Consequently, the idea of song selection took on an entirely new gravity. It was during this season that I was introduced to a song called "Held."

It was written by Christa Wells and includes the stories of three phenomenal women. One was a young widow with three children. One was a mother who had overcome polio as a child, and then lost her baby unexpectedly in infancy. The third was a woman who carried her baby to term, only to have to say goodbye in the delivery room.

I can't comprehend the pain that each of these women experienced—nor the integrity that they displayed. Each woman demonstrated a level of faith and surrender that defied human instinct. The grace they embodied was the work of the divine.

As Christa allowed their stories to penetrate her heart and culminate in a work of inspired redemption, a song was born that would go on to touch many lives. The lyrics recounted the pain of loss—the death of family members, of children, and the resulting confusion of deciphering God's presence in it all. Our brokenness seems to consume every part of us. But God's presence takes precedence if we simply allow Him to hold us close.

> *This is what it means to be held*
> *How it feels, when the sacred is torn from your life*
> *And you survive*
> *This is what it is to be loved and to know*
> *That the promise was when everything fell*
> *We'd be held*

This song came to me shortly after my time in India. In Mumbai, God helped me discover the truth of my calling. He impressed upon me the command to live, speak, sing, love differently. When I surrendered myself and took on a new calling, God walked with me. He led me to songs that would never again be "Natalie Grant" songs. He led me to HIS songs which cried out to be sung in the key of hope, grace, and peace.

A JOYFUL NOISE

I'm not the only one to experience a profound transition in career and calling. We find a remarkable biblical example in Paul, who experienced a dramatic awakening and received a new song. Even before his conversion, Paul was an esteemed orator. He was a leader in the church. Yet before he came to faith, he facilitated and oversaw the murders of early Christians.

In Acts 9, we read of the moment of his conversion:

> Meanwhile, Saul was still breathing out murderous threats against the Lord's disciples. He went to the high priest and asked him for letters to the synagogues in Damascus, so that if he found any there who belonged to the Way, whether men or women, he might take them as prisoners to Jerusalem. As he neared Damascus on his journey, suddenly a light from heaven flashed around him. He fell to the ground and heard a voice say to him, "Saul, Saul, why do you persecute me?"
>
> "Who are you, Lord?" Saul asked.
>
> "I am Jesus, whom you are persecuting," he replied. "Now get up and go into the city, and you will be told what you must do."

> The men traveling with Saul stood there speechless;
> they heard the sound but did not see anyone. Saul got up
> from the ground, but when he opened his eyes he could
> see nothing. So they led him by the hand into Damascus.
> For three days he was blind, and did not eat or drink
> anything. (Acts 9:1–9)

If you recall, God asks one of his disciples in Damascus, Ananias, to find Saul and restore his vision. With reason, Ananias balks a bit. Who blames him? God is sending him to a known persecutor of Christians. Yet, in faith, he obeys. He finds Saul.

Ananias had to be terrified. But he exhibits no ill will, judgment, or even a hint of retribution when he meets a man who would have gladly killed him a few hours earlier.

Now, imagine you're Saul. You're blind, in a city you don't know, hungry and thirsty. You don't know that God's going to end the blindness and enfold you in the arms of loving people. All you know is who you have been and what you have done—oh, and now you're a part of the thing you thought you hated.

True to what he was commanded, Ananias baptizes Saul, restores his sight, and helps set him on a path that would change the world in the name of Christ. So begins Paul's new chapter in life. He's operating from a new perspective. He's been given a new song.

> Saul spent several days with the disciples in
> Damascus. At once he began to preach in the synagogues
> that Jesus is the Son of God. (Acts 9:19–20)

I can't wrap my mind around verse 20. At once he was back in the synagogue. He didn't go on a retreat or take a sabbatical to adjust himself to this radically new way of life. He didn't put a public relations plan in place to soften the blow of his transition from one side to another. As bold and direct as God was on the road to Damascus, so too was Saul as he embarked on this new life.

The only explanation lies in verse 15. He was God's chosen instrument: "But the Lord said to Ananias, 'Go! This man is my chosen instrument to proclaim my name to the Gentiles and their kings and to the people of Israel.'"

You too are God's chosen instrument. You have a voice fine-tuned by the heavens, and God knows exactly where you need to be. Like Paul, it may seem to be exactly the opposite location, vocation, or message than you had planned . . . but when God gives you a song, no power on earth can drown it out.

That's not to say that it's going to be easy. Verse 16 makes that clear: "I will show him how much he must suffer for my name."

Still, Saul, who would become known as Paul, did not live a life of misery. He was persecuted, yes. He was booed off the stage. His life was threatened. He suffered for God's name. But he demonstrated a joy that defies common sense. Consider when he and Silas were (unjustly) beaten and thrown in jail; they didn't sit around bemoaning their circumstances. "About midnight Paul and Silas were praying and singing hymns to God, and the other prisoners were listening to them" (Acts 16:25).

Soon, their song had caught the attention of the guard, who was so astounded at their faith that he helped them escape. Their songs of praise in a jail cell had set them free, given new life to a prison guard, and liberated the other prisoners. What a testament to the power of a song! In the freedom of his true voice, in allegiance to his One True King, Paul had joy.

As you flex your voice and joyfully share it with the world, there is no critic, no judge who can ever demean or denounce what you have to share. Circumstances might make it difficult to hear at times. Some might try to silence or take advantage of your voice, but the truth remains: Your God-given song contains echoes of eternity and can change lives in an instant.

Finding and using your voice is not about fame. It's not about success. It's not about eloquence, perfection, or even popularity. The truth is, the brightest spotlight on the greatest stage goes dark without the light of the world: love.

If I speak in the tongues of men or of angels, but do not have love, I am only a resounding gong or a clanging cymbal. If I have the gift of prophecy and can fathom all mysteries and all knowledge, and if I have a faith that can move mountains, but do not have love, I am nothing. If I give all I possess to the poor and give over my body to hardship that I may boast, but do not have love, I gain nothing.

Love is patient, love is kind. It does not envy, it does not boast, it is not proud. It does not dishonor others, it is not self-seeking, it is not easily angered, it keeps no record of wrongs. Love does not delight in evil but rejoices with the truth. It always protects, always trusts, always hopes, always perseveres.

Love never fails. But where there are prophecies, they will cease; where there are tongues, they will be stilled; where there is knowledge, it will pass away. For we know in part and we prophesy in part, but when completeness comes, what is in part disappears. When I was a child, I talked like a child, I thought like a child, I reasoned like a child. When I became a man, I put the ways of childhood behind me. For now we see only a reflection as in a mirror; then we shall see face to face. Now I know in part; then I shall know fully, even as I am fully known. And now these three remain: faith, hope and love. But the greatest of these is love. (1 Corinthians 13:1–13)

Even when everything around you seems to muffle or extinguish your words, you have a heavenly Father who hears every syllable, every thought, every fear, everything your voice has ever uttered. He will not leave you or forsake you or silence you. You're part of a chorus of women, daughters of God called to lives of love and purpose—and He has a melody picked out just for you. He has given you a song that no one else can sing. You are precious and beloved to Him, His chosen instrument to speak truth, light, and love to a broken world.

Believe in who you are and what you have to say. Trust the potential and abilities God has uniquely placed within you. Find your range and embrace your thrive zone. Take care of yourself—your whole self—as your instrument for which God has great purposes.

So grab a blank page and start writing a new song. Kick out shame and hurt. Make room for hope and courage. Aim for trust, not doubt. Choose faith over fear. Because the Savior knows your name and calls you His own, you can rise above any circumstance. As you open your mouth and raise your voice, you will drown out the lies with the melody of this truth: you are a daughter of the King. That is enough. He is enough. You are enough.

As your life begins to soar on that melody, others will join the chorus.

And I, for one, can't wait to sing along.

ACKNOWLEDGEMENTS

To Caroline Lusk—Thank you for helping to bring my voice to life. This book would never have become reality without you.

NOTES

Chapter 1: *Learning to Listen*

1. http://www.child-development-guide.com/speech-development.html.

Chapter 5: *Caring for Your Instrument from the Inside Out*

1. Centers for Disease Control and Prevention, "Insufficient Sleep Is a Public Health Problem," http://www.cdc.gov/features/dssleep/.
2. Kate Harris, *Wonder Women* (Grand Rapids: Zondervan, 2013).
3. Gina Shaw, "Women and Weight Training for Osteoporosis," http://www.webmd.com/osteoporosis/living-with-osteoporosis-7/weight-training.
4. "What Is the Lifespan of a Voice?" *Discovery News*, Feb. 17, 2012, http://news.discovery.com/human/voice-singing-whitney-houston-120217.htm.

Chapter 6: Aligning Your Assets

1. Rudie Obias, "15 of the Most Requested Karaoke Songs," April 22, 2013, http://mentalfloss.com/article/49789/15 -most-requested-karaoke-songs.

Chapter 7: Quality Check: It's How You Say It

1. Stuart Wolpert, "In Our Digital World, Are Young People Losing the Ability to Read Emotions?" *UCLA Newsroom*, Aug. 21, 2014, http://newsroom.ucla.edu/ releases/in-our-digital-world-are-young-people-losing -the-ability-to-read-emotions.